BASEBALL SUPERSTARS

Mariano Rivera

✦✧✦✧✦✧✦✧✦✧✦✧✦✧✦✧✦✧✦✧

Hank Aaron

Johnny Damon

Lou Gehrig

Derek Jeter

Andruw Jones

Mickey Mantle

Albert Pujols

Mariano Rivera

Jackie Robinson

Babe Ruth

Ichiro Suzuki

✦✧✦✧✦✧✦✧✦✧✦✧✦✧✦✧✦✧✦

✶✶✶✶✶✶✶✶✶✶✶✶✶✶✶✶✶✶✶

BASEBALL SUPERSTARS

Mariano Rivera

Judith Levin

☑Checkmark Books®
An imprint of Infobase Publishing

✶✶✶✶✶✶✶✶✶✶✶✶✶✶✶✶✶✶✶

For Brian, who taught me to love baseball.

Checkmark Books
An imprint of Infobase Publishing
132 West 31st Street
New York NY 10001

Library of Congress Cataloging-in-Publication Data

Levin, Judith (Judith N.), 1956-
  Mariano Rivera / Judith Levin.
    p. cm. — (Baseball superstars)
  Includes bibliographical references and index.
  ISBN 978-0-7910-9599-7 (hardcover)
  ISBN 978-0-7910-9901-8 (pbk)
  1. Rivera, Mariano, 1969—Juvenile literature. 2. Baseball players—Panama—Biography—
Juvenile literature. I. Title. II. Series.
  GV865.R496L48 2008
  796.357092—dc22
  [B]   2007040545

Checkmark Books are available at special discounts when purchased in bulk quantities for businesses, associations, institutions, or sales promotions. Please call our Special Sales Department in New York at (212) 967-8800 or (800) 322-8755.

You can find Chelsea House on the World Wide Web at http://www.chelseahouse.com

Series design by Erik Lindstrom
Cover design by Ben Peterson

Printed in the United States of America

Bang EJB 10 9 8 7 6 5 4 3 2 1

This book is printed on acid-free paper.

All links and Web addresses were checked and verified to be correct at the time of publication. Because of the dynamic nature of the Web, some addresses and links may have changed since publication and may no longer be valid.

CONTENTS

1   Mo the Unhittable   1

2   Childhood in Panama   9

3   Rivera in the Minor Leagues   19

4   Champions: Mariano Rivera
    and the 1996 Yankees   31

5   The Glory Years (Minus One):
    1997–2000   54

6   The Year They Lost: 2001   67

7   "Not the Same Team": 2002–2006   87

8   2007 and Beyond: Rivera's Legacy   101

    Statistics   112

    Chronology and Timeline   113

    Glossary   117

    Bibliography   120

    Further Reading   124

    Index   126

Mo the Unhittable

In the beginning of 2007, after a strong spring training and four games without giving up an earned run, Mariano Rivera faltered. On April 27, after blowing two saves in a row, the Yankee closer's ERA was 12.15. Rivera said what he had always said when he hit a bad patch: that he was fine, that no one had any reason to worry about him. Manager Joe Torre himself went to the mound to remove Rivera in one game. "How often have you seen *that*?" exclaimed a commentator, obviously shocked. Not often. What everyone *had* seen often—but forgets each time—is the immediate panic that occurs when Mo Rivera gets hit.

It is true that Rivera's slump in the beginning of the 2007 season was bad. One of the blown saves lost a game in which Alex Rodriguez had hit two home runs. It is true that Rivera

New York Yankees manager Joe Torre *(third from left)* took reliever Mariano Rivera *(third from right)* out of a game on April 27, 2007, against the Boston Red Sox. Rivera suffered a slump early in 2007, and the fans and the media reacted as they generally did when Rivera went through a bad spell—they panicked.

looked worried. Two weeks later, when Rivera allowed a two-out, ninth-inning homer to Seattle, he lost his cool and yelled, "Oh my God" as the ball exited the stadium. The man with ice water in his veins had shown his feelings on the mound. He had also lost the game for his team.

In an article in the New York *Daily News*, he admitted:

> It's easy when everything goes fine, [but] you show your true character when you struggle like this. I don't know what people are thinking about me, but I know I feel the same way as I did last year and the year before. I feel real good, the velocity is there. It's nothing I have lost, it just happens. If you are a closer, you're going to blow saves and get saves. There's no in between. I feel I'm being tested right now, my character, my faith, how I conduct myself. It's different. But I love it. If God allows this test to be on me, hey, I'm willing to carry it. We are just starting; we'll see where we finish. I'm going to battle. . . . I believe I'll finish strong.

Several factors seemed to be contributing to Rivera's difficulties. "Pitching is finesse, and if you don't do it constantly, you will lose it," he said. The Yankees were not presenting him with save situations, where he would have to come in when the game was on the line, so he was not working enough. Sometimes he was called in just so he could get some work, but without the pressure of the save situation. Even more than with other pitchers, a closer's routine and discipline are important to him, because a relief pitcher must come to the mound and perform immediately, without any time to settle in. Rivera had always been "robotic" in his preparation, but he had had a decade of preparing for save situations and now he was being called in to pitch when the Yankees had a bigger lead and the pressure *wasn't* on him the same way.

Finally, as Rivera slumped, he lost some of his intimidation factor. For 11 years, he had been the unhittable Mariano. Now, a batter would look at Rivera's recent appearances and think, I *can* hit this guy. You could see it on their faces, in their stances at the plate. You could see how Rivera moved, tentatively, without some of the grace that he had had for a decade.

Every time that Rivera had slumped in his career, even briefly, there had been a general panic. Someone would say that batters had finally learned to hit him, or, more recently, that he was getting old. (For a closer, 37 is old.) "Rivera No Longer Mr. Automatic" said a newspaper headline—in 2002. Then it turned out that he still was.

The Rivera of spring training and the first games had been the same old Mo, focused, graceful, efficient, and unhittable, and that Rivera would return—his ERA for the month of June would be 1.98. One measure of Rivera's greatness is how startled everyone is when he is not perfect and not in perfect emotional control. A Rivera slump? "It's something that I don't want to think about," said Torre—but he said it in 1996.

"ENTER SANDMAN"

When Mariano Rivera stands on the pitcher's mound, baseball fans might notice that he is small for a modern pitcher, 6 feet, 2 inches (188 centimeters) and slender. He is quiet for a closer, and eerily calm. You cannot tell if he won the day before or lost. You cannot tell how he is feeling. He has none of the strut and swagger, the taunting looks or challenging stares that many pitchers cultivate. Rivera does not like that behavior. He thinks pitchers who behave that way are showing disrespect for the game or for themselves. It shows that they are afraid. He has chosen to have an emotionless game face: He does not want the players on the other team to think he is showing them up. Scout Billy Blitzer says, "Mariano doesn't come in to intimidate you. He says, 'Here's what I've got. Go beat me.'"

Rivera isn't afraid. He looks intense, but he's just focused—so focused that the rest of the stadium might as well not be there. He says, "In the ninth inning, when the game is on the line, if you start listening to all these people"—the 50,000-plus screaming fans—"forget about the game. You're gonna lose." He is aware only of the hitters, or sometimes just the target made by the catcher's mitt. Nothing else exists in that moment.

☆ ☆ ☆ ☆ ☆

THE PERSONALITY OF THE RELIEF PITCHER

Although Mariano Rivera does not quite fit this mold, relievers have traditionally been "swaggering intimidators." They have to be fearless, have great arm control, a 95-mile-per-hour (153-kilometer-per-hour) fastball or some sort of specialized pitch, and a short memory. They need to be able focus entirely. They seek an adrenaline rush. A starting pitcher can take an inning or two to settle down; a reliever cannot, especially when he is called in because the starter is in trouble. In *Pen Men*, an oral history of relief pitching, author Bob Cairns adds to those requirements "an offbeat sense of humor" to balance the stress.

Some relievers have been very odd indeed. Al Hrabosky, the "Mad Hungarian," who played from 1970 to 1982, wore a half-beard. Sparky Lyle, who was with the Yankees in the 1970s, kept many of his loonier antics—sitting naked on birthday cakes, for example—off the field. Many have glared, spat, stomped, and threatened.

It's a hard job. Relief pitchers cannot afford a single mistake. Everyone is watching while they perform an intensely difficult task. Relief pitcher Lefty Gomez once said, "A lot of things run through your head when you're going in to relieve in a trouble spot. One of them is, 'Should I spike myself?'"

Closer Mariano Rivera is known for his focus and his intensity. When he enters a game, his only thoughts are on the batter he is facing and on getting that batter out. Here, Rivera delivers a pitch in the ninth inning of the Yankees' 7-6 win over the Minnesota Twins on July 5, 2007. In that game, Rivera recorded the 424th save of his career, which tied him for third all-time.

He does not think about yesterday's win or loss or if he is on a streak.

Of course, Rivera does not have to intimidate the batter. He just throws the ball—his one pitch, a nearly unhittable cut fastball that breaks sharply over the plate—and the batters are intimidated. He places it with such precision that even though batters know what he is going to throw, that knowledge does not help them. It drives the other teams crazy. "Ban him from baseball. He should be illegal," said Tom Kelly, the Minnesota Twins' manager, in 1996, Rivera's first full season in the major leagues. His pitches splinter so many bats that hitters often choose not to use a favorite bat against him. Opposing teams dread his entrance, his light jog to the mound accompanied (when he's in Yankee Stadium) by his theme music, Metallica's "Enter Sandman." The song's lyrics say, "Sleep with one eye open, gripping your pillow tight." It is a song about having a nightmare, and for batters, Rivera is it.

Of course, for the Yankees, he is a dream come true. They breathe a sigh of relief: Mo's here. Game over. Lights out. So, the few times he has failed them have been memorable, including Game 7 of the World Series against the Diamondbacks in 2001. Still, since 1996, Rivera's success has been nearly a sure thing, and he has the statistics to prove it. Even when he has failed, and failed badly, he shakes it off. He is almost as unflappable as he is unhittable. He has no fear of failure, say teammates and coaches. Nothing scares him.

Being the closer is a high-pressure job. The closer is the relief pitcher who specializes in closing the game—or getting the final outs. Since a closer usually appears with the game on the line, he is generally the team's best reliever. The closer is "the hero or the goat," says Goose Gossage, who was a Yankee closer in the late 1970s and early 1980s and who was a bullpen coach when Rivera came up from the minor leagues in 1995. Rivera bears the pressure well, partly because of his physical skills and partly because of his attitude.

Rivera says he works hard and he's lucky. He's lucky to be a baseball player and lucky to have a strong arm and good health. He says that, if he had not become a baseball player, he probably would have been happy as an auto mechanic, because he likes cars. A devout Christian, he says he is in God's hands. He is humble, grateful, and completely sure of himself, without being arrogant. He is also funny, though that does not show when he is pitching. He says of his job, "I get the ball, I throw the ball, and then I take a shower." Rivera's career as a Yankee includes the years from 1996 to 2000, when the team won four World Series in five seasons. It also includes the years since then, when they have made the play-offs each season but have not been able to win a single World Series. Yet, although the team and its success rate have changed, Rivera has changed very little—even with his remarkable career and his "rags to riches" life story.

Childhood in Panama

Mariano Rivera was born on November 29, 1969, in Panama, that skinny country where North America and South America come together and just barely touch. Half the country faces the Caribbean Sea, and the other half faces the Pacific Ocean. That is the side that Mariano Rivera grew up on, in the town of Puerto Caimito, west of Panama City and the Panama Canal.

CARDBOARD BASEBALL GLOVES

As a boy, Mariano played baseball with his friends and his cousins on the beaches, streets, and vacant lots of their town. They had no real fields or leagues. They did not have much equipment either. Someone might have a real baseball—they played with it until it fell apart and then covered it with tape so that it could still be used. Otherwise they rolled up an old T-shirt or a piece of fishing net with a rock in the center and taped it. Bats and gloves were even sketchier. The boys used sticks for bats or—if they were lucky—a piece of a sawed-off broomstick. The boys made their own gloves, too, taking a piece of cardboard or a juice container and folding and bending it so that it protected their palms but still had some flexibility.

Baseball in Mariano's childhood was not like baseball on a Little League team. He and his friends had no equipment, no fields, no adult coaches. It was the kind of baseball that was played in New York City from the 1930s through the 1960s, when boys played stickball in the streets. The boys played—nearly every day in Panama, which is near the Equator so it has no winter—for fun, not for trophies or tournaments. Unlike stickball in New York or baseball as played in some other Latin American countries, the young Panamanian ballplayers did not spend much time imagining that they would be discovered by a scout. Although Rod Carew played in the major leagues from 1967 to 1985 and became the first player from Panama to be inducted into the Baseball Hall of Fame, baseball is less the national game than soccer is. Mariano's childhood sports hero was the Brazilian soccer star Pelé.

Even though Mariano played baseball for fun, he played to win. If his side lost, he wanted to play again, right away. He was, he says, fiercely competitive. When, at age 10, his father gave him a real leather glove, he took it with him everywhere—to school, to church, and even to bed. Sometimes his mother hid it, saying he would pay better attention in school without it.

THE RIVERA FAMILY

Rivera speaks with love about his childhood home. It was, in terms of cash or opportunities, a poor childhood and a hard one. Puerto Caimito is only about 30 miles (48 kilometers)

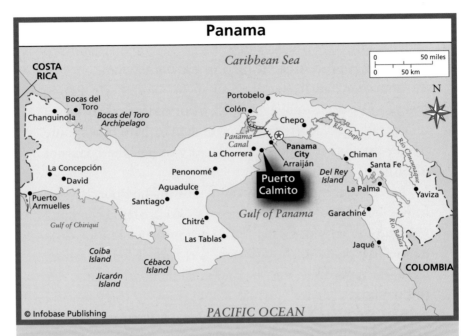

Panama

Caribbean Sea

0 — 50 miles
0 — 50 km

N

COSTA RICA

Bocas del Toro
Changuinola
Bocas del Toro Archipelago

Portobelo
Colón
Chepo

Panama Canal
La Chorrera
Panama City
Arraiján

Río Chepo

Chiman
Santa Fe

Puerto Calmito

La Concepción
David
Penonomé
Aguadulce
Santiago

Del Rey Island
La Palma

Yaviza

Puerto Armuelles

Gulf of Chiriquí

Chitré

Gulf of Panama

Garachiné

Río Balsas

Las Tablas

Jaqué

Coiba Island
Cébaco Island
Jicarón Island

COLOMBIA

© Infobase Publishing

PACIFIC OCEAN

Mariano Rivera grew up in Puerto Caimito, Panama, on the Pacific coast. Many of the people in this town of 7,000 make their living through fishing—either catching sardines out at sea or processing them in the local factory. Mariano's father was the captain of a fishing boat.

from Panama City, but it seems farther away. The Rivera family's house, like the houses of their neighbors, was a small one made of concrete with a corrugated tin roof. People raised chickens in their yards.

Although the beach was only about 100 feet (30.5 meters) from his house, Puerto Caimito was not a resort town. "Puerto" means "port," and the town of 7,000 or so people had one main industry. The men and the older boys went out on 130-ton commercial fishing boats and used nets to catch sardines, which they sold to the town factory. There, the sardines were ground into meal that was used in animal feed. The work was hard and dangerous. A boat and its fishermen might go out and catch tons of sardines in a few hours, or it might take 24 hours.

Sometimes the boats stayed out for days. For all of this work and risk, the men earned about $50 a week. People who worked in the factory processing the fish made about the same.

Mariano's father was the captain of one of the fishing boats, and people called him "Captain Mariano." It was a title of respect. The Riveras, though, did not have much more money than other families. The factory owned the boat, not Mr. Rivera.

Rivera does not complain about growing up poor. He says he was lucky. "I love Panama," he says. "We are family people." Mariano has an older sister, Delia, who was named for their mother. Mariano, as the first son, was named for his father. Delia was responsible for Mariano's childhood nickname, *Pile* (pronounced "pee-lee"), which some people in the town still call him. She said "Mariano" was too long. After Mariano came two brothers, Alvaro and Giraldo, but even before they were born (and grew big enough to play with), Mariano had cousins living nearby. "Family" in Panama, as in many Latin American countries, means extended family, and the Riveras had plenty of relatives close by. One of them, Mariano's cousin Rubén, would become a Yankee soon after Mariano did.

Mariano Rivera has never talked much to reporters about his family. He believes that his personal life is private. When he talks about his father, though, he generally says the same thing: that as a boy he wished his father would go easy on him, "give me a break," but that now he is glad his father was strict. His father demanded respect. He insisted that there was a right way and a wrong way to do things. He taught his children to face the consequences for their actions. Rules were clear, and rule-breaking—or breaking a window with a baseball—would result in a spanking.

"STRONG MIND"

Opposing teams, teammates, fans, and sportswriters look at Rivera's pitching—his focus, his ability to put mistakes

Mariano Rivera and his father joked around for the camera in this photo taken in 1997. Rivera says that his father's expectations gave him the poise he now has on the mound. "His character is strong, and he taught me to be that way," Rivera said about his father.

behind him, and his physical skill—and wonder how he does it. Rivera believes that his father's expectations and rules gave him self-discipline, self-assurance, and confidence, and helped turn him into the man who calmly faces down hitters in the ninth inning in the postseason. "If it wasn't for him, I don't think I would have this character. His character is strong, and he taught me to be that way." Although little is known about Rivera's childhood, it is possible to look at the child he was and see the man he became. He had that in-born competitiveness—the little boy whose response to defeat was to play again rather than to withdraw. He had (and has) the confidence of a winner—like teammate Derek Jeter, for instance, he expects to win, expects to play well, and believes he can do it. Even as a child, he had pride in what he did. When girl cousins or their friends watched the boys play, Mariano wanted to do well so that they would not laugh at him. Of course, no one wants to be laughed at, but giggling girls would make Mariano lift his chin and play better, rather than make him self-conscious or nervous. Focusing under pressure came naturally to him, and he also developed it. He says—as his father would—that what is important is a "strong mind."

The young Mariano also had a liking for order ("I like to be neat," he says) and a willingness to do something over and over again until he could do it well. His father demanded that he apply himself to tasks, but his father did not tell him to spend hours throwing a rock or an old ball at a target. Mariano wasn't even a pitcher—he played all positions—he just enjoyed mastery, control, and the process of improving a skill. He liked to tinker with objects and says he could easily have grown up to be a car mechanic because he likes cars and likes to figure out how things work and make them work better. Instead he grew up to tinker with his throw, with how his hand held and released a baseball.

MARIANO GROWS UP

In high school, it was soccer, not baseball, that Mariano played seriously, and if he had dreams of playing a sport professionally, he dreamed of soccer. Soccer drew on and improved his natural athleticism. He was always quick, graceful, and aggressive, and he has fast feet. What he did not have, as it turned out, was strong ankles, and a series of injuries and chronic ankle pain persuaded him that he had no future as a soccer player.

In his teens, Mariano did not know where his future lay. After leaving high school at 16, he worked on his father's fishing boat. He learned that he did not have it in him to follow in his father's footsteps as a ship's captain or even as a fisherman. He became even more sure of this after he survived a near-disaster at sea, when a 130-ton boat full of fish capsized. He and the rest of the crew were able to scramble to safety onto another boat, but Mariano decided all over again that he was not meant to be a fisherman. He respected his father's work, but it was "way too tough."

GETTING SCOUTED

At 18, Mariano played amateur baseball on a team called *Panamá Oeste* (Panama West). The team was good enough to make it to the national championship, where Mariano was spotted by a native Panamanian named Herb Raybourn, who was scouting for the Kansas City Royals. It was 1988 and Mariano was a shortstop—a 6-foot 2-inch, very skinny shortstop. Raybourn noticed him but was not impressed. Rivera had a good arm, but he did not bat brilliantly and did not seem strong enough.

The following year, *Panamá Oeste* again made it to the national tournament, but the team's pitching became so bad that Mariano, the shortstop with the good arm and the childhood habit of throwing objects at a target, said he would pitch. A couple of the players on Mariano's team thought his pitching was so good that they spoke to Yankee scout Chico Heron about him. Two weeks later, Mariano was in Panama City at a Yankee tryout camp. Heron was there, and so was Raybourn, who was now in charge of Latin American scouting for the Yankees. Raybourn recognized the skinny shortstop from the year before. He watched Mariano throw only nine pitches before he said he had seen enough. Heron thought that Raybourn was not interested, but actually Raybourn had made up his mind quickly. Mariano was throwing only 85 to 87 miles per hour (137 to 140 kilometers per hour), but he threw with great accuracy. Raybourn did not know if Mariano could make it in the majors, but he liked the accuracy of Mariano's pitches and his general athleticism. Raybourn saw a player who was entirely untrained and much too thin. He suspected that a diet and exercise program designed to put some weight on him along with pro coaching would put extra speed on the throws. Coaching, too, would teach Mariano to throw different pitches. Raybourn

★ ★ ★ ★ ★

BASEBALL IN LATIN AMERICA

Baseball has been called "America's pastime," but maybe that should be "Americas' pastime," because the game has been played in parts of Central and South America since the 1800s. In nations like Brazil, Argentina, and Chile, soccer is king, but in the countries that ring the Caribbean—Venezuela, Mexico, Panama, Nicaragua, and Colombia—and on the islands of Cuba, Puerto Rico, and the Dominican Republic, *béisbol* is a passion.

Many baseball fans know that Cuba's Fidel Castro became a political leader only as his second career choice. What he really wanted to be was a baseball player. Cubans learned to play baseball in the middle of the 1800s, when the game was young even in the United States. At that time, college students, businessmen, and American sailors traveled freely between the United States and Cuba, and Cubans—first the upper class and then everyone— fell in love with the new sport. It seemed modern and excitingly American to a people who were growing tired of their Spanish rulers. The Spanish outlawed the sport and imprisoned one of its stars, which, of course, only made the game more attractive.

People in other nations in the region also learned to play baseball. Wealthy students sent to the United States to study brought the game home; American sailors played it with longshoremen. But it was the Cubans who spread baseball most signed Mariano as an amateur free agent. Mariano received a signing bonus of $2,000. The next year, Mariano suggested that the Yankees look at his younger cousin Rubén, an amateur center fielder. Rubén was signed for $3,500.

Mariano says that he never thought about being a major-league player until he was signing the contract in his living

★ ★ ★ ★ ★

widely. Baseball scout Oscar Fuentes said, "The Cubans were the missionaries of baseball. They spread it like it was a religion, like the friars spread the Catholic faith in the days of the conquistadors." Many Cubans left the country during a war against Spain that lasted from 1868 to 1878 and settled, for instance, in the Dominican Republic.

In the early 1900s, owners of sugar plantations in the Dominican Republic supported the growth of baseball teams for their workers, who faced a six-month period each year when little work needed to be done with the sugarcane. Baseball seemed a safe, cheap way to keep the workers entertained. It was a kindness to them but also served the owners' needs.

The Caribbean nations developed their own amateur and professional baseball leagues, and many still exist. The "Caribbean Series" was begun in 1949 and played until 1960 among the professional teams of Cuba, Panama, Puerto Rico, and Venezuela. The Cubans won seven times, but then the Cuban revolution took place and Castro banned professional baseball. When the Caribbean Series was begun again in 1970, it was—and still is—played by teams from the winter leagues in the Dominican Republic, Mexico, Puerto Rico, and Venezuela. The modern series is played by major-league players and prospects.

room. "I was surprised by everything," Rivera said later. "Usually a player prepares for years. Here I was signing, and I wasn't even a pitcher." He knew he had a huge opportunity but was also taking a risk. He was leaving all that was familiar—his home, his family and friends, and his girlfriend, Clara. He spoke no English. His mother cried. He cried. His father neither encouraged nor discouraged him. It was his, Mariano's, decision to make, but if he was going to take this opportunity, he had to do it right—he had to work hard and not waste energy being homesick.

So, on February 17, 1990, Mariano Rivera became a Yankee.

Rivera in the Minor Leagues

We imagine the great Mariano Rivera coming to Yankee Stadium, coming from his fishing town to New York City. Of course, that's not what happened. He had been signed as a pitcher, but he was not a pitcher—he was a skinny guy who had thrown rocks at a target as a boy. So he went to a rookie league in Tampa, Florida: the Gulf Coast League, for players who are not even ready for Class A ball. The squad included pitcher Andy Pettitte. In the minors, Rivera would play with many of his future teammates, including Jorge Posada and Derek Jeter.

ROOKIE LEAGUE

The rookie league in Tampa was not a bad place for Rivera to be. He knew he needed to work on his skills, and he had to get used to living in a new country, without his family. He arrived in the United States not speaking any English. There were Spanish-speaking players and a Spanish-speaking community, so—although the league provided an English teacher—Rivera did not even try to learn the language. (This, he soon learned, was a mistake.)

He did, however, succeed as a pitcher. In 22 appearances (only one of which was a start), he allowed 1 run in 52.0 innings, for an ERA (earned run average) of 0.17. He gave up only 17 hits and 7 walks. On August 31, 1990, he pitched a seven-inning no-hitter against Bradenton, for which, he reminded the coaches, he was due a $500 bonus. He was named the Gulf Coast League "Star of Stars," an award given for the best overall performance. Glenn Sherlock, who managed the Yankees' team in the Gulf Coast League in 1990 (and would see Rivera again in 1995 as the Yankees' bullpen catcher), admired the young pitcher. In a league from which only a small percentage of players ever make it to the major leagues, Sherlock saw Rivera as calm, professional, and competitive. Rivera was quiet and tough and wanted to win, and he seemed older than his age of 20.

In 1991, Rivera advanced to Class A ball, playing in Greensboro, North Carolina, and wishing he had learned English the year before. There was no Spanish-speaking community in Greensboro then and no Spanish-speaking players on his team, either, he says. Years later, he said of his year in Greensboro, "It was just me. It was tough. I cried every day, not because I was lonely but because I couldn't communicate with anyone. I told myself I had to learn English." He shopped and cooked for himself, which he enjoyed, and hung out with his teammates, more or less throwing himself on their mercy. "I told the players, 'I know you guys will laugh at me and that's fine, as long as you tell me the right way [to speak].'" Rivera survived with an ERA of 2.75 in 29 games

Derek Jeter talked to Mariano Rivera as Rivera came in to pitch in the eighth inning of the first game of the 2004 American League Championship Series against the Boston Red Sox. Rivera and Jeter— along with other players like Andy Pettitte and Jorge Posada—all came up together through the Yankee farm system in the early 1990s.

(15 starts). Now, however, he tells young Latin American players to learn English quickly.

Rivera was learning English, but there was no question that Panama was still home. Between seasons, he went back, to be with his family and—on November 9, 1991—to marry Clara, the young woman he had been dating since they were teenagers.

When Rivera returned to the United States for the 1992 season, he was still in Class A ball, but in Fort Lauderdale, which was in a Class A-Advanced league. Of the players on the Yankee minor-league teams, Rivera was rated (by *Baseball America*) as the ninth-best—his cousin Rubén was first, Derek Jeter was second, and Andy Pettitte was third. Rivera was doing well, but he wanted to develop a wider range of pitches. A medium-fast fastball and a changeup were not going to get him to the majors. Rivera began to fiddle with how he threw, trying to snap his wrist to see if he could produce a breaking ball. His experiments resulted in his needing surgery. On August 27, 1992, Dr. Frank Jobe repaired nerve damage in Rivera's elbow.

Elbow surgery is bad news for a pitcher, but for Rivera his elbow repair turned out to be good luck and good timing. A few months after Rivera's surgery, Major League Baseball held its expansion draft to fill the rosters of its two newest teams, the Colorado Rockies and the Florida Marlins. The Yankees could protect only 15 players from the draft, and they would not have protected Rivera, who had not proved himself yet. Because no one was sure how well he would recover from the surgery, however, neither of the new teams wanted him either. During spring training in 1993, he played catch with retired stars Whitey Ford and Ron Guidry to work his arm back into shape. Then he returned to Class A ball in Greensboro.

Rivera's minor-league managers in 1993 and 1994 loved his attitude and admired his skills. "This guy is our best outfielder," Brian Butterfield, the manager at Greensboro, said, describing Rivera fielding balls during batting practice.

Mike DeJean, a relief pitcher who played with Rivera during that time, said later, "I never saw him get mad. I never saw him sweat. When he pitched, it was like he was acting as if he were the only guy on the field. Even then you could see the easy mechanics and how the ball just exploded out of his hand. But more than anything else, you could see Mariano had quiet confidence." In 1993, when Rivera was still playing Class A ball, Yankees general manager Gene Michael put Rivera on the team's 40-man roster (which includes inactive players) to protect him from trades. Michael's eye for developing talent led him to protect other minor leaguers during the early 1990s, including Derek Jeter, Bernie Williams, Jorge Posada, and Andy Pettitte.

MOVING UP IN THE MINORS

In 1994, Rivera finally was promoted. He was sent to the Class AA Albany-Colonie Yankees on June 5. As early as his Albany games, sportswriters were beginning to notice him. "Mariano is a pitching coach's dream," began one article. They noticed, as always, both his skills and his attitude. "I know I can pitch," he said. "It's no big deal. I try to do my best." He did lack a "brushback" pitch, the article noted. Then, as now, Rivera felt no need to intimidate the batter.

On July 22, he was promoted to the Class AAA Columbus Clippers. This promotion was especially welcome. Not only was this level of ball within sight of the majors, but at this level the players begin to be treated like pros. Rivera said later of the minors, "They make it tough so that you'll hurry up and make it to the big leagues." Rivera was never going to complain about getting to play baseball for a living, but he did not enjoy the long (sometimes 10- to 12-hour) bus rides between games or the fast-food hamburgers of A and AA ball. Triple-A players traveled by plane.

But if Rivera was already very much himself as a man and a teammate, as a pitcher he was not yet the Mo who was the unstoppable, unbeatable, unhittable, "Game Over" player of a few years later. He was not a relief pitcher yet, either. As a Class AAA starter with six starts, he achieved an ERA of 5.81.

☆ ☆ ☆ ☆ ☆ ☆

LATINOS IN MAJOR LEAGUE BASEBALL

Since the earliest days of baseball in Latin America, players have come to the United States to play on professional teams. In 1871, before the modern era of baseball, a Cuban named Esteban Enrique Bellán played for the Troy Haymakers. After 1900, the first Latino player was the Colombian Luis Castro, who played one season—1902—with the Philadelphia Athletics. Other Latin American players followed, though only some could play in the major leagues. Others, of equal talent but with darker skin, were banned from Major League Baseball and played in the Negro Leagues until baseball was racially integrated in 1947.

The movement between countries did not just involve Latin American players coming to the United States. Professional play-ers from the United States joined Latin American teams in the off-season to earn extra income or to practice their skills. Players from the Negro Leagues discovered that they could be paid better and treated with more respect outside the United States.

As early as the 1930s, the Washington Senators had scouts in Latin American countries, and during World War II, teams raided Caribbean nations for players to replace the major leaguers who had gone to war.

After Jackie Robinson became the first African-American major leaguer, the big leagues were open to Latin Americans no mat-ter what their skin color. Hundreds of players came to the United States, including Humberto Robinson, one of the first players from Panama. He was with the Milwaukee Braves and the Philadelphia Phillies from 1955 to 1960. Another player was the Panamanian

Then, a strained left hamstring kept him off the mound for 10 days in the beginning of August. It still was not clear if Rivera had what it took to become a major-league pitcher. His pitches

★ ★ ★ ★ ★

Rod Carew, who played from 1967 to 1985 and was elected to the Baseball Hall of Fame in 1991, the first year he was eligible.

By the 1980s, many major-league teams not only had scouts in Latin American countries but they also had begun to develop young players in baseball academies. These are especially numerous in the Dominican Republic, which is sometimes called "The Republic of Baseball." Years ago, a Dominican winter-league manager, Winston Llenas, said of baseball, "It's more than a game. It's our passion. It's almost our way of life." The academies serve both the Dominican players and the American franchises, although perhaps not equally. Players coming to the academies at 17 are fed well, housed well, and trained well. Many have not had showers, indoor toilets, or balanced meals before. They have played, as the young Mariano Rivera did, with cardboard gloves and rag or stone balls. At the academies, they have a chance to learn and to try to fulfill a dream: to come to the United States and be a rich baseball player. Yet many of the boys have left school as young as 10 to practice baseball full time, hoping to be the next Sammy Sosa or Pedro Martínez. About 98 percent never make it to the majors and have developed no other skills.

Although the major leagues are seeing increasing numbers of players from Japan and other Asian countries, players from Latin American countries or of Latin American descent now make up about 25 percent of the major-league teams. In the early 1990s, Rivera found himself the only Spanish speaker on one of his minor-league teams. That will probably never happen again.

still did not have the range or the velocity a starter would need. His fastball never broke 90 miles per hour (145 kilometers per hour), and generally it was slower. Still, Yankee manager Buck Showalter said later, "The thing I liked about his minor-league numbers was his lack of walks—and his athleticism." Showalter also admired his "presence." Looking at Rivera's strikeout-to-walk ratio in the Gulf Coast League (58-7) and at Greensboro in the Southern League in 1991 (123-36), Showalter said, "That is impressive in any league. This guy is going to make it." At that time, he had never seen Rivera play—he was just looking at his numbers.

BIG-LEAGUE DEBUT

In May 1995, Rivera's AAA manager, Bill Evers, phoned to tell Rivera that he had been called up to pitch for the New York Yankees. Some pitchers were injured, and Rivera was needed. At first, Rivera thought Evers was kidding him. After he realized this was no joke, he hung up the phone and jumped up and down on his bed with excitement. Then he called his family in Panama.

The great Mariano Rivera had arrived. Well, not yet. Not only did he lose his first game, but in his first four starts for the Yankees, Rivera had an ERA of 10.20. By June 11, Rivera had been sent back down to Class AAA Columbus, and Gene Michael was considering trading Rivera to the Detroit Tigers for a starter named David Wells. During this time, Rivera made one start for Columbus, then went out with a sore shoulder, which may have accounted for his poor starts.

THE FASTER FASTBALL

What happened next cannot be explained by anyone in baseball. It is "one of the amazing mysteries of the game," Brian Cashman, who became the Yankees general manager in 1998, said later. On June 26, 1995, Rivera pitched a five-inning no-hitter against the Rochester Red Wings that was called on account of rain. His catcher, Jorge Posada, said the Red Wings had "no chance."

Somehow, from somewhere, Rivera had come up with a reliable 95- to 96-mile-per-hour (153- to 154-kilometer-per-hour) fastball. "Super Mariano" was on his way.

When Gene Michael reviewed the reports of the game the next day, his first thought was that the speed gun was broken. Evers, the Columbus manager, said the gun was working just fine. Still unable to believe that, overnight, Rivera had suddenly added several miles an hour to his fastball, Michael called a friend who had been at the game. Hiding his true interest (his friend was looking for players to recruit to the St. Louis Cardinals), Michael managed to extract the information he had been seeking: yes, Rivera really had been throwing 95 mph, and no one could touch his fastball. Michael had Showalter call Rivera back up as a starter.

Where did Rivera get that fastball from? He was always a hard worker, his elbow surgery was a year and a half behind him, and he was a grown man, not an 18-year-old who might have suddenly gotten stronger. Rivera believes the faster pitch was a gift from God. Cashman and Showalter guessed that it had taken longer than expected for Rivera to get over his surgery. The fastball, though, was there to stay.

A "SMASHING START"

On July 4, 1995, Rivera struck out 11 White Sox players, his eight-inning shutout marred only by a run let in by closer John Wetteland. "Rivera May Have Said Final Goodbye to Columbus" said the headline of a *New York Times* article about Rivera's "smashing start." Rivera had been able to carry his recent minor-league record ($20^2/_3$ innings without allowing a run) seamlessly into the major leagues. "I pitched just like I did in Columbus," Rivera told the *Times*, "and it worked." The element of surprise had helped him. The scouting report had told the White Sox that Rivera threw about 85 or 86 mph

(137 or 138 kph). Yet, as always, Rivera's mental toughness helped, too. "It's not easy, but I did it," he said. "'It's just another batter. It's just another hitter.' That's what I told myself. It worked."

But, in fact, Rivera was not yet finished with the minors. He was back in AAA and started two games there in August, then was recalled to the majors. In what would turn out to be the last start of his professional career, against the Mariners, he gave up five runs in 4²/₃ innings. Although Rivera would later hope for another chance as a starter, his terrible outing against Seattle was the end of Rivera's career as a major-league starting pitcher. For the remainder of the 1995 season, he was a bullpen pitcher with no clear role, one who barely made it onto the postseason roster. During the season, Rivera had appeared in 19 major-league games, nine of them in relief. His regular-season ERA was 5.51.

THE POSTSEASON

The Yankees made it to the postseason as the American League wild-card team. It was the first year of the wild-card berth, which had been designed to add an extra round to postseason play. In the first round, the Yankees were matched up against the Seattle Mariners in the American League Division Series. They won the first two games at home and then lost the next three away, in Seattle's old Kingdome, and that was the end of their season. It was during that series, though, that Rivera first emerged as the great postseason reliever, the pitcher with "ice water in his veins," as Goose Gossage described him.

Rivera had been yo-yoing up and down between the minors and the majors all season. Sometimes he was great, but he had been uneven. Buck Showalter did not look at a tight situation and say to himself, "We need Mo here." He wasn't Mo yet—he was just Rivera, a pitcher without a role. Even doing great relief in the 1995 postseason, he was not yet a big story. He won Game 2, at home, pitching 3¹/₃ scoreless

New York Yankees pitcher David Cone bent over in exhaustion after he walked in the tying run in the eighth inning against the Seattle Mariners in Game 5 of the 1995 American League Division Series. Cone was pulled from the game, and Mariano Rivera came in with the bases loaded. Rivera struck out the next batter to end the inning—one of the first signs of Rivera's prowess as a postseason reliever.

innings. In Game 3, he disposed of four Mariners without giving up a hit, but Randy Johnson's pitching won the game for Seattle. Gene Michael noted, "I think we've found someone here." Derek Jeter, who—though not yet a major leaguer—was sitting on the bench during the postseason, was not surprised at all by Rivera's performance. "I knew it from the minor leagues. I knew what Mariano could do," he said. Rivera had faced 16 batters in the postseason and had an ERA of 0.00.

Then came Game 5, the rubber game of the five-game series. In the eighth inning, an exhausted David Cone threw his 147th pitch of the game and walked in the tying run. Rivera came in with the bases loaded and two outs. He faced Mike Blowers, who at the time was a .420 hitter with the bases loaded—the tensest situation possible for a pitcher and the sort of situation that does not call for a rookie. Rookie pitchers have been destroyed by challenges like that one: They fail and they never get their nerve back again. "I know what people were probably thinking then," Rivera said later: "Who is this guy?"

Rivera struck out Blowers with three pitches. Blowers went down looking. Showalter then replaced Rivera after he retired one batter in the ninth inning. The Yankees would go on to lose the game in the eleventh inning, and with it, the series. What if Showalter had left Rivera in? Would the Yankees have made it to the World Series that year? "I don't know what would have happened. No one knows," Rivera says.

That face-off between Rivera and Blowers is what many reporters and players mention as the moment when they realized the kind of pitcher Rivera would be. It was not solely what he had done, but the way he looked when he did it. Years later, David Cone said he remembered thinking, "Welcome to the stratosphere, kid." Goose Gossage, watching the game on television, looked at Rivera's face and saw no fear. In a situation of maximum pressure, there was no evidence of stress on Rivera's face or in his body. He was loose, focused, and tough—the qualities that would make him the reliever and closer he became.

Rivera said, "I did my job, but we lost, and I was feeling devastated, but I learned a lot and I kept that with me."

Champions: Mariano Rivera and the 1996 Yankees

It's not news that Yankee Stadium was home to some of the greatest dynasties in baseball history—teams that won for years, passing the World Series title on each year as a ruling family passes on a crown. From 1923 to 1962, the team won 20 World Series. In the 1955 musical *Damn Yankees*, an old Washington Senators fan sells his soul to the devil in exchange for one season as a brilliant young player who can lead his team to victory over the hated Yankees.

In 1996, though, the Yankees had not won a World Series since 1978. After their 1981 World Series loss to the Los Angeles Dodgers, the team had not won the American League pennant again. The Yankees were an unsuccessful team. They weren't even worth hating.

THE BEGINNING OF THE STEINBRENNER ERA

When George Steinbrenner (with a group of other investors) bought the team in 1973, he built a team that *was* worth hating, but a long drought followed their 1977 and 1978 World Series wins. Steinbrenner could buy expensive players, but he could not buy a *team*. Managers came and went, quickly. Some managers, like Yogi Berra, were fired after only a few weeks. Steinbrenner earned a reputation as the worst boss in baseball.

And of course, Steinbrenner consistently failed to do what he most wanted to do, which was to win. He would not let his managers manage or let his players jell as a team. Aside from being impatient and mean, he failed to understand baseball as a game. He behaved as though he owned a football team. A single loss threw him into a furious panic, as if one game was going to decide the season. But the baseball season is a long one, and if players and managers cannot put lost games and losing streaks behind them, they are not going to survive. Steinbrenner's approach—yell, fire someone, or tell the newspapers that a player is a "fat, pussy toad"—did not improve the morale or playing ability of his team. By the 1980s, some players and managers refused to work for Steinbrenner.

In 1990, the Yankees were awarded the first pick in the June 1991 draft of new players, an "honor" given the team that has the worst record. Also in 1990, baseball commissioner Fay Vincent handed Steinbrenner a lifetime suspension from baseball for having tried to buy information from a gambler to use against one of his own players, Dave Winfield, whose contract he wished to break. The suspension was revoked after two-and-a-half years, but during that time Steinbrenner could not hire and fire players or managers or tell them how to do their jobs. Given two-and-a-half years of peace, the team started to turn around.

George Steinbrenner, the Yankees' owner, is shown leaving the office of baseball commissioner Fay Vincent in July 1990, after Vincent banned Steinbrenner from baseball. Because of the ban, which lasted two-and-a-half years, Steinbrenner was not involved in the operations of the Yankees. The team seemed to benefit from Steinbrenner's absence.

GENE MICHAEL AND BUCK SHOWALTER

Steinbrenner had hired Gene Michael as the general manager who would control the team in his absence. After the 1991 season, Michael hired Buck Showalter as manager. Michael had a good eye for developing players, and he rebuilt the Yankees' minor-league teams, producing a farm system that "grew" a number of the players who would be critical to the 1996 team. (Steinbrenner wanted proven winners, not young hopefuls.) Mariano Rivera, Derek Jeter, Jorge Posada, Bernie Williams, Andy Pettitte, and Mariano's cousin Rubén Rivera were all products of the farm teams. Additionally, Michael wanted players to think about building a run for the team, not just about individual stats or hitting home runs. (Steinbrenner liked home runs.)

Buck Showalter managed the Yankees for four years, the longest anyone had held the job since Steinbrenner bought the team, and he used that time to build a team that worked like a team. When he watched videos of games, he looked not only at individual performances but also at how players functioned as part of a team. Did they jump off the bench to watch a ball that a teammate had hit to right field? (You can't see right field from the Yankee dugout.) He also improved conditions for players in the stadium, renovating the weight room and creating a room where the players' young children could play during games.

Showalter worked such long hours that sometimes he slept in his office. In 1994, he was named Manager of the Year, and the Yankees had the best record in the American League East. The season, though, had ended early when talks between baseball management and the players union failed and the players went on strike in August. No World Series was played in 1994.

In 1995, the Yankees won the American League wild card but lost the division series to Seattle. At the end of the season, a number of contracts expired. These included the contracts of Showalter and Michael and several of the team's senior players: first baseman Don Mattingly, third baseman Wade Boggs, pitcher David Cone, and catcher Mike Stanley.

Showalter and Michael had built a solid, successful team, but they had not won the World Series for The Boss. Steinbrenner offered Michael a new contract—with a pay cut. Michael refused. Steinbrenner then offered to make Michael director of scouting, which Michael accepted. (It was a less pressured job and one that involved doing what he liked best.)

Steinbrenner negotiated with Showalter while telling him that he would have to fire his coaches and cut the payroll. Showalter signed a contract to manage the Arizona Diamondbacks, an expansion team so new that he would be able to help design its uniforms and playing field. One feature of that design would come back to haunt the Yankees in 2001.

THE BEGINNING OF THE JOE TORRE YEARS

Steinbrenner hired Bob Watson as general manager and Joe Torre as manager. Torre had been an All-Star Gold Glove catcher but had never played on a team that made it to the play-offs. He had also been the manager of teams that had not made the play-offs. Then he worked as a radio broadcaster. When Steinbrenner hired Torre, the press made much of Torre's failures as a manager. Mike Lupica, a sportswriter for the New York *Daily News*, called him "Clueless Joe."

Gene Michael believed that Torre's teams had lost because they were not good teams, not because Torre was a poor manager. Also, Michael knew what it was like to work for Steinbrenner, and he believed that Torre's laid-back managerial style would be helpful to the team. Torre wanted the job. Even more than most players and managers, Torre longed for a World Series ring. His older brother, Frank, had played in two World Series and won one. Torre figured that the job of Yankee manager was his last shot at the World Series. Of course, he had heard all the stories about Steinbrenner, but he concluded that at least he would be working for an owner who wanted to win as badly as he did. He said that the worst Steinbrenner could do was fire him—he couldn't shoot him.

"I'M THINKING WORLD SERIES"

Torre startled the New York press early in spring training by announcing that he expected the team to go to the World Series. "I really like our chances," he said. Torre was sticking his neck out. Steinbrenner would fire a manager who did not

Before the 1996 season, the Yankees hired a new manager, Joe Torre *(left)*, and a new general manager, Bob Watson *(right)*. In his years as a player, Torre had never made the play-offs. Early on, he said that the Yankees would make it to the World Series—a bold prediction.

deliver on a promise. It was an early indication that Torre would be Steinbrenner-proof.

Actually, Torre wasn't at all sure that the team could make it to the World Series. The 1995 team had been turned upside down, and he could not know how his collection of old players and rookies would perform. The off-season hirings had Steinbrenner's fingerprints all over them. Don Mattingly had retired. Mike Stanley, an essential member of the 1995 team, had been ignored. When no one even called him to discuss his contract, he figured he should get a job somewhere else. Randy Velarde, another old standby, was gone, too. Then, having threatened Showalter with the need to lower his budget, Steinbrenner had signed first baseman Tino Martinez for $9 million more than Martinez and his agent were even asking. He replaced Stanley with Joe Girardi at catcher. Some experienced players remained, though, including Paul O'Neill and Wade Boggs.

The young players who were part of the 1996 team have become so famous that it is hard to remember how inexperienced they were that spring. Pettitte had been a rookie the year before. Posada was a rookie, on the bench as the team's third catcher. Bernie Williams had been in center field for two-and-a-half years. Twenty-one-year-old rookie Derek Jeter had been told in the off-season that he could play shortstop, but then he went 0-for-11 in the beginning of spring training and made fielding errors. So the team was partly old stars and partly guys who were rookies, or at least young. One of these young players was Mariano Rivera.

PITCHING UPS AND DOWNS

In 1996, the Yankees either had a lot of great pitching or not nearly enough. The team had hung on—barely—to star David Cone. Steinbrenner had signed pitcher Dwight Gooden, who was coming off a year-and-a-half suspension for drugs. No one could know if he would stay clean or if he could still pitch. (During spring training he couldn't.) Steinbrenner signed pitcher Kenny Rogers. (Many people believed that Rogers was a great pitcher but not a great pitcher for a New York team.) He was injured in spring training, although he kept it a secret. Jimmy Key had had four shoulder surgeries. Pettitte, at least, had been strong in 1995, his rookie year.

Rivera's place in the bullpen remained unclear to Torre. Rivera had been so good in the 1995 postseason that Bob Watson had said he was "untouchable." At least one general manager told Watson that he would give anything to get Rivera, but Watson turned him down. "Mariano is going to be here for a long, long time," Watson said. Closer John Wetteland had already told Rivera that he should think about becoming a closer. "You have the stuff to do it," Wetteland said.

But it wasn't so clear to Torre. Rivera still had one pitch: a 93- to 95-mile-per-hour (150- to 153-kilometer-per-hour) fastball that sometimes moved and sometimes didn't. In spring training it didn't, and Torre told Watson that he should consider offers for Rivera. To Torre, Rivera looked to be some sort of middle reliever, but the team already had side-armer Jeff Nelson, the aging Steve Howe, set-up man Bob Wickman, and closer John Wetteland.

The many Yankees who had been in the minors with Rivera could have told Torre how good Rivera was. Jeter said, "He had one pitch in A-Ball, and no one hit it. No one hit it at Double-A. No one hit it at Triple-A. Now it is the majors. There is no place else for him to go. They just aren't going to hit it."

THE "JUICED BALL" THEORY

Twelve games into the season, the Yankees were 6–6, and it was too early to tell how (or if) the team was coming together. Fans were booing Girardi and Martinez because of whom they had replaced. Rivera had nearly frozen during the home opener, played in the snow. It was already clear that the season would turn out to be a hard one for pitchers. Something had—perhaps—been done to the ball after the 1994 strike, and people spoke, wrote, and invented conspiracy theories about a "juiced" ball, a ball that had been wound tighter to make hits carry farther and to liven up the game. Other explanations for the high number of hits and the record-breaking number of homers included "juiced" players (players on steroids) and the number of new fields with shorter outfields. Whatever the reason, in April 1996, pitchers across the majors were being hit often and hit hard. They were throwing more pitches and running up pitch counts, and they were being relieved early—and Joe Torre's pitching rotation and his bullpen were not as strong as he had hoped.

RIVERA'S (WEEK-LONG) NO-HITTER

When the Yankees faced the Minnesota Twins on April 19, starting pitcher Dwight Gooden gave up six runs in three innings. The Yankees lost 7-1 but saw a hint of what was to come, as Rivera struck out five batters and gave up no runs in pitching three innings of relief.

In Kansas City on April 22, starting pitcher David Cone noticed that he had no feeling in the middle finger of his right hand and his hand stayed cold no matter what he did. He was able to pitch successfully, but after five innings, he was through. Nelson, Howe, and Wickman had pitched the day before, so Torre sent Rivera in, and Rivera pitched three perfect innings before Wetteland came in to close.

The Yankees took on the Twins on April 26. Kenny Rogers was pulled at the top of the sixth inning, with the Twins leading, 4-0. Rivera came in to face the heart of the batting order, with runners on first and second and no outs. Rivera walked the first batter (future teammate Chuck Knoblauch) and then retired the next three batters. In the bottom of the sixth, the Yankees collected five runs, four of them on a grand slam by Bernie Williams. Rivera then pitched two perfect innings, and Wetteland saved Rivera's win.

The Yankees faced the Twins again on April 28, and after five innings, starting pitcher Jimmy Key left the Yankees behind 3-2. Rivera's three innings were marred only by another walk to Knoblauch, and the Yankees produced the necessary runs to give Rivera a win, saved in the ninth inning by Wetteland.

Rivera's "no-hitter" caused Torre, Rivera's teammates (those who didn't already know him from the minors), and Yankee fans to take notice of him and his stats. He had gotten 29 outs over 10 innings without giving up a hit, and his ERA

Mariano Rivera threw a pitch during the sixth inning of a game on April 28, 1996, against the Minnesota Twins. He pitched three hitless innings in this game—part of a stretch of relief appearances in which he threw 10 no-hit innings. The fans, the press, and opposing teams began to take notice of Rivera.

for the season stood at 1.37. The newspapers called Rivera "unhittable," but he told *New York Times* reporter Claire Smith, "It's not that I feel unhittable, I just feel comfortable." He added, "From last year, I keep a lot of confidence in myself. I can throw with no doubts. I just do my job."

It was at this time that Torre began to realize what he had in his bullpen and to decide what to do with him. The answer, in 1996, was to use Rivera as the setup man for closer John Wetteland—not usually for three innings, but for two. The team's starters struggled, but Rivera could influence the outcome of the game several times a week, not just as part of a five-man rotation.

Rivera did not yet have his signature pitch—the cut fastball. The one pitch he did have in 1996, however, was sometimes called a cutter. This pitch kept surprising people: He was so slender, and his delivery was so smooth, and the ball almost always looked hittable and almost always wasn't. The Yankees backup catcher, Jim Leyritz, said, "A couple cutters he threw to me were pretty nasty, and the hitters were looking at me and asking when he started throwing this. He threw a pitch to Molitor [Paul Molitor of the Twins] that he missed by a foot. We've never seen that. Usually he throws hard but straight. Now his ball is moving."

THEY DO TALK ABOUT RELIEVERS

Rivera would have preferred to be a starter and said he still hoped to be one, but he added that, of course, he just wanted to help the team and that any role that allowed him to pitch was fine. Ten years later, he was still saying it: "They talk about starters," he said. "They don't talk about relievers." Rivera himself would make this statement untrue. Rivera made the role of reliever more high-profile, even more glamorous, than it had ever been. The 1996 season and especially the postseason demonstrated for all times the importance of relief pitching, writer Roger Angell would conclude.

And people certainly did talk about Mariano Rivera. "Super-Mariano," newswriter Rafael Hermoso called him. By the end of May, Jack Curry, one of the top sportswriters with the *New York Times*, had written an article about Rivera called "The Indispensable Yankee." Joe Torre called Rivera the team's "most indispensable pitcher." Rivera was 3-0 with a 0.83 earned run average. He had two saves (earned while he was closing when John Wetteland was on the disabled list), 33 strikeouts, and 11 walks in 32²/₃ innings.

☆ ☆ ☆ ☆ ☆

RELIEF PITCHING

Before 1891, a starting pitcher could not be relieved unless he was injured or sick. If his pitching became bad enough, he might switch positions with a player already on the field.

The "bullpen" was originally the roped-off area where fans could come in late and stand and watch the game for 10 cents. Relief pitchers (if any) warmed up alongside them. In 1904, about 90 percent of all games were finished by the starting pitcher. Gradually, though, teams, including the New York Highlanders (who would become the Yankees), began to use relief pitchers, sometimes referred to back then as "the heroic saver."

Until the 1920s and '30s, a relief pitcher was usually an old starter or a young and unproven wannabe. The position was generally not a specialty, although the Washington Senators' Fred Marberry is considered the first great pitcher to be used primarily in relief. In 1925, Marberry appeared in 55 games without starting any.

As late as 1950, Branch Rickey (the Brooklyn Dodgers general manager who hired Jackie Robinson) said in a memo: "You know how I feel about relief pitchers. I don't believe in them. . . . They are simply necessary evils."

Jack Curry called him "dominant," "overpowering," and "superb" but also "soft-spoken," "genuine," and "humble." Rivera read his Bible in the clubhouse and sent boxes of baseball equipment to children in Panama. Ozzie Guillén (of the White Sox) said Rivera was "the finest pitcher in baseball."

During the 1996 season, the Rivera-Wetteland team was nearly unbeatable. If the Yankees were ahead after six innings, they won. This was critical to the season, in a year when middle relief was getting hit hard. The team could almost think of it

☆ ☆ ☆ ☆ ☆

In the 1960s, managers began to use "ace relievers" to introduce a fresh arm (and a pitcher the other team was not used to), even if the starting pitcher was not in trouble.

The 1970 season was the first time that there were more saves recorded than complete games. The "ace reliever" would go in as a "fireman" to extinguish rallies. As relief pitching became common, it also became specialized, with short relievers, long relievers, middle relievers, setup pitchers, and closers.

Long relievers are pitchers who traditionally enter a game early when the starting pitcher cannot continue. Middle relievers are also called upon when several innings of work are required, though they typically come in during the sixth or seventh innings. Short relievers are used in the late stages of a game when the team has a lead or a reasonable chance of winning.

The setup pitcher regularly appears just before the closer, commonly in the seventh and/or eighth innings. And the closer is the pitcher who specializes in getting the final outs in a close game.

as a six-inning game. Then, as Tino Martinez said, it was the "Mo Show."

A DIFFERENT KIND OF TEAM

Steinbrenner complained that the 1996 team was not the old Bronx Bombers. In a year when home-run records were being broken, the Yankees, with Torre's help, were turning themselves into a different kind of team. Bob Watson would later say that the games that set the tone for the season were the first two games against the Baltimore Orioles, a hard-hitting team in a home run-friendly stadium.

Game one, on April 30, was the longest nine-inning game in major-league history—4 hours and 21 minutes. The Yankees struggled against a strong Orioles team that included Roberto Alomar and Cal Ripken. Starting pitcher Andy Pettitte was removed in the second inning, when he was unable to get an out against the first six batters. He would be charged with nine runs. Jeter had gone 0-for-15 before the game, and Martinez and Girardi had been hitting badly, too. The Yankees, though, battled back, forcing the Orioles to remove their starting pitcher in the fifth inning and go to their shaky middle relief. Jim Leyritz then hit a two-run homer to tie the game. The Yankee relievers allowed only one run, and Torre brought Rivera in to pitch hitless seventh and eighth innings—he was in a hitless streak, now at 35 at-bats. Tino Martinez hit a three-run homer to break the tie. The game would end with the Yankees ahead, 13-10, with closer John Wetteland throwing the 400th (and last) pitch of the game. It was the biggest come-from-behind victory for the Yankees since August 1993.

The Yankees were in first place in the division. They would remain there for the rest of the season.

In the second game against the Orioles, on May 1, the Yankees made errors but fought back, and took advantage of Oriole errors. Pettitte, like Rivera, took losing as a personal challenge and after his embarrassing and brief appearance on

April 30, Pettitte told Torre that he wanted to get right back in the game. By the twelfth inning, Rivera (who was supposed to have the night off) found himself warming up in the bullpen next to Pettitte. "That," said Rivera, "was crazy." Torre put Pettitte in for the thirteenth and fourteenth innings and—in the top of the fifteenth inning—Martinez hit a grand slam and Gerald Williams got his sixth hit of the game and an RBI. Pettitte finished off the Orioles with a scoreless fifteenth inning and an 11-6 victory.

"Those were two games I'll never forget," Joe Torre said afterward. "People asked about our leadership and what kind of ball club we were going to be. But after these two games I don't think anybody can question the chemistry, class, and ruggedness of this team." It was, sports columnist Joel Sherman said, "the moment when the Yankees of Joe Torre showed that no game, no series, no season was ever over."

"I'M ONLY HUMAN"

Early in May, Rivera missed a game with a sore shoulder. "I'm only human," he told reporters. It's a point he has to make from time to time, but it's one that people never quite believe and certainly one they do not want to hear. "The Yankees never saw a clearer illustration of the dual world in which they exist than Saturday's 11-5 blowout by the White Sox," wrote reporter Bob Klapisch for *The Record*. "There's the Rivera reality—where all manager Joe Torre has to do is pick up the bullpen phone and wait for Rivera to turn fastballs into dots. And then there are days when Rivera is unavailable, like Saturday, when Torre's best strategy is prayer." There were two problems: the tattered state of the starting rotation, which led Torre to have to call on the bullpen early, and the unreliability of the relief aside from Rivera's "voodoo."

Rivera's unhittable streak ended in his next game. After Chuck Knoblauch's hit against him in Minnesota on April 19, he was not hit again until May 5 (against the White Sox) and

the crowd at Yankee Stadium gave Rivera a standing ovation—*before* the scoreboard prompted them. Rivera does not
listen to the crowd, he pays attention to his pitching. "I never
thought about the streak," he said, but, still, "I feel good about
it"—about the cheering. "It makes me feel they were following
the game, following me."

By June 5, 1996, the *Star-Ledger* said of Rivera: "He's a
weapon. But he's certainly not a secret anymore." A Rivera loss
would have teammates and journalists shaking their heads in
disbelief. At the end of May, he strained his back on Oakland's
high pitcher's mound. After that injury, Rivera allowed runs
in five of his next eight appearances. On June 28, Rivera gave
up his first home run of the season, and Torre had to pull
him from the game (he had allowed three runs). Rivera was
philosophical. "I have to take it," he said. "I expect to do the
job every time out. I'm the kind of guy who says if I didn't do
the job, I accept it. I tried my best, but things happen. That's
baseball. I feel OK about it. This is not the end."

ALL-STAR GAME

In mid-season Rivera suffered a disappointment that was
greater than his loss of a game. In early June, Torre said he
would call whomever he needed to in order to make sure
Rivera had a place on the All-Star team. There was no place,
however, on the roster for a middle reliever. Going into a
series with Boston at the beginning of July, Rivera had a 1.96
ERA, lower than any starter in the American League. Rivera
had tried to prepare himself for the disappointment. "I'm
ready for the worst," he said before the team was announced,
"but growing up, I've always wanted to be an All-Star, just
once." He obviously would be on an All-Star team eventually,
but not that year. Instead, he would visit friends in Tampa
and then be ready to play against the Orioles and the Red Sox.
"That's the most important thing, winning, making sure we
stay in first place."

Yankees manager Joe Torre hugged Mariano Rivera after the team clinched the American League East title on September 25, 1996. The Yankees had won the division for the first time since 1981.

DIVISION CHAMPS

On September 25, the Yankees clinched their spot in the play-offs. The team won the American League East for the first time since 1981.

For Rivera, the regular season ended on September 28. Having started the season as a tradable, maybe-middle-reliever, he had established himself as one of the most important players on the team. He had broken Goose Gossage's team relief record of 122 strikeouts, getting 130 in 107 ^{2}/$_3$ innings of play. He had allowed only one home run all season.

The key to postseason pitching was going to be getting to the seventh inning with a lead and then turning the mound over to the Rivera-Wetteland team. During the regular season, the Yankees were 70–3 when leading after the sixth inning and 79–1 when leading after the seventh inning: The Rivera-Wetteland formula was nearly unstoppable.

DIVISION SERIES

In the first round of the play-offs, the Yankees faced the Texas Rangers, an unfortunate match-up. The Yankees were 1–5 for the year at The Ballpark in Arlington. They had been outscored there 44-15. To have any chance, they at least needed to win their first two games at home, because the final three games were to be played in Texas. Instead, they lost the first game.

Game 2, with Pettitte on the mound, looked as if it was going to be another loss. With one out in the seventh inning and the Rangers ahead 4-2, Torre put Rivera in the game. This was only the third time that year that Torre had used Rivera when the Yankees were behind, but he hoped that Rivera's magic would turn the game around. Rivera got eight outs with only 25 pitches, and the Yankees were able to work their way back into the game. In the twelfth inning, with Derek Jeter on second base, Charlie Hayes hit a bunt. Dean Palmer, the Rangers' third baseman, fielded the rain-slick-ened ball and overthrew first base, allowing Jeter to come in for the winning run.

In Texas, the Yankees overcame their regular-season trouble and were able to win Games 3 and 4. The third game required a ninth-inning comeback and relief pitching from Jeff Nelson. (Rivera did not play that day.) In Game 4, the Yankees trailed 4-0, and starter Kenny Rogers had to be pulled after only two innings. In their third come-from-behind win, the Yankees used four relief pitchers, one of whom was Rivera, who pitched two innings and gave up no hits. Of the 15 batters he had faced in the division series, Rivera had given up one walk and no hits. The series marked the beginning (aside from his one inning in 1995) of Rivera's reputation as the greatest postseason closer of all time.

AMERICAN LEAGUE CHAMPIONSHIPS

The Yankees next faced the Baltimore Orioles in the American League Championship Series. The opener (and perhaps the entire series) is best remembered for an incident of fan interference that turned around the game. With the Orioles leading 4-3, Derek Jeter hit a fly ball that was intercepted by the glove of 12-year-old Jeffrey Maier at the fence in right field. (Most fans know his name; fewer know that he dropped the ball.) Umpire Richie Garcia saw the ball vanish but did not see Maier's glove. He ruled the hit a home run. The win belonged to Mariano Rivera, who pitched innings 10 and 11 of the game, giving up three hits but no runs.

The angry Orioles, still protesting Garcia's bad call, won the second game in Yankee Stadium, and the series moved to Camden Yards. There, in Game 3, for the fifth time in the play-offs, the Yankees came from behind to win.

The Yankees were ahead 8-4 in Game 4 when Rivera entered in the seventh inning. Back in 1996, the Orioles could hit Rivera, and in the bottom of the eighth inning, he gave up three singles in a row, with nobody out. He then got two strikeouts and a pop-up and handed the ninth to closer John Wetteland.

When the Yankees won Game 5, they were in the World Series for the first time since their loss in 1981.

The Orioles' assistant general manager said, "I think we had better players than the Yankees, but they had the better team. Their whole approach to the game was just more determined. We had a group of superstars, while the Yankees kept coming and grinding and pressing." That determination and that sense of being a team is what Torre had wanted and had helped to create: "A team like this is a rarity. This team wasn't concerned about numbers, only winning. We used all the ingredients—that's what glued us together."

THE WORLD SERIES

The Atlanta Braves, the Yankees' opponent in the 1996 World Series, were the defending World Champions. They were media mogul Ted Turner's high-salaried team, and they were the ones to beat, as the Yankees had been in the past. The Yankees were not quite underdogs, but baseball fans had been hearing an awful lot of the Braves' tomahawk chant for the last few years.

In the last three games of the National League Championship Series, the Braves had outscored the St. Louis Cardinals 32-1. In the first two games of the World Series, the Yankees could not hit the Braves, and they could not outpitch the Braves, either. The Braves took the first two games in Yankee Stadium, 12-1 and 4-0.

The starter in Game 3 was David Cone, who pitched six innings, allowing only one run. Rivera came into the game in the seventh. He pitched $1^1/_3$ innings and let a run score before he was taken out in the eighth inning, but the Yankees won 5-2.

Game 4 was the game that turned the Series around. After five innings, Atlanta led 6-0. The Yankees scored three runs in the sixth inning but quickly went down in the seventh inning. So many Atlanta fans believed that the game (and probably the Series) was over that they went home, chop-chopping with their foam-rubber tomahawks as they left the stadium. But in the eighth inning, with two men on, Yankees back-up catcher Jim Leyritz faced relief pitcher Mark Wohlers. Wohlers threw a slider that hung over the plate, and Leyritz knocked the ball over the left-field fence, making the score 6-6. In the tenth inning, Braves pitcher Steve Avery walked Wade Boggs with the bases loaded to force in the seventh run. The Braves' substitute first baseman, Ryan Klesko, then lost the ball in the lights only moments after taking the field, allowing the eighth run. Wetteland closed out the game. It was one of the greatest comebacks in World Series history, second only to a game in 1929 when the Philadelphia A's rallied from an 8-1 deficit. Rivera, who had allowed two hits in $1^1/_3$ innings, was one of 13 pitchers used by the two teams during the game. The game had been his third in three days, and he had a sore shoulder. Torre had not wanted to use him.

Pettitte shut the Braves down in Game 5, in a game closed out by Wetteland. The team's postseason record on the road was 8–0, and it was time to come home for the end of the Series.

The Yankees had October 25 off as a travel day, and—with the Hollywood timing that seemed to have scripted much of the 1996 season—that is the day that Joe Torre's brother Frank received the new heart he had been waiting for since the beginning of the play-offs. By the evening of October 26, he was in intensive care but able to watch Game 6. "This really was like a fairy tale," one of his doctors said.

The Game 6 pitchers' matchup was the Braves' Greg Maddux—whom the Yankees had tried hard to sign—against the Yankees' Jimmy Key. Maddux was the better pitcher, but "he made a few mistakes and we took advantage," said Bernie Williams. Torre brought in relievers David Weathers and Graeme Lloyd in the sixth inning but, Weathers said, "all we wanted to do was get the game to Mariano." Having finally had two days' rest, with the World Series on the line, Rivera walked the first batter he faced and then got six straight outs. In the ninth inning, Wetteland allowed three singles that brought in a run before the Braves' Mark Lemke popped up a ball that landed in Charlie Hayes's glove for the last out of the last game of the 1996 World Series.

Mariano Rivera's determination is apparent as he pitches in Game 6 of the 1996 World Series. Rivera pitched two innings of relief. After walking the first batter, he retired the next six over the two innings. The Yankees beat Atlanta, 3-2, to win the game and the World Series.

RIVERA'S FIRST WORLD SERIES

Rivera's own ovation had come when he left the field after the eighth inning, cheered loudly by fans. In the postseason, he had allowed one run in 14 $1/3$ innings, even after being used for too many days in a row. His combined ERA for the regular season and the postseason was 1.92. His meaning to the team went beyond his numbers. Until the postseason, the bullpen had been dreadful, and Rivera had been the one reliable—nearly magically reliable—middle reliever. Catcher Joe Girardi would later say, "When I think of 1996, I think of Mariano Rivera."

Rivera came in third in votes for the Cy Young Award, which had never been won by a setup man. He was twelfth in the voting for the American League Most Valuable Player— higher than any other Yankee. The Yankees had not had outstanding individual stats—it was as a team that they were champions. "There's no column on the official stat sheet for magic," Tom Verducci wrote. "In '96, everyone was Mr. October." In 2006, Rivera said of the 1996 team, "Basically we didn't have the superstars we have now, but we had 25 players that were hungry to win a championship."

Rivera, like his teammates, was elated by the win against Atlanta and by the experience of the ticker-tape parade up lower Broadway in Manhattan. He always says that this World Series win, his first, is the one he treasures the most. But pressed to say what day was most memorable, he says November 3—the day he arrived home in Panama. In New York, hundreds of thousands of fans turned out to see the parade, while at the airport in Panama there were only hundreds, but Rivera said, "It was just like New York. I had never seen New York like it was the day we had the parade. It was the same thing here [at the airport in Panama]. I think everyone in Panama was there. It was unbelievable. That made me feel they were in New York with me."

The Glory Years (Minus One): 1997–2000

John Wetteland's contract expired after the 1996 World Series. As good as he was, team management felt that, at $4 million, he was too expensive. Rivera, who had earned $131,125 in 1996, could do the job. Rivera was given a raise—to $550,000—and the promotion to closer.

RIVERA BECOMES YANKEE CLOSER

Even after Rivera knew that the team was letting Wetteland go, he was surprised to find out that he was going to be the closer. He was pleased to be stepping into a more visible position. "I have no doubt I can do the job," he said. "I'm sure I can do it." It is often the setup man who has the harder job, but the closer gets the save and the glory. As good as Rivera had been in 1996, there had not been a spot on the All-Star team for him.

Rivera would miss Wetteland, who signed with the Texas Rangers as a free agent. A player often resents the team member likely to replace him, but Wetteland had helped and taught Rivera. Rivera was sad to lose a friend from the team yet said he understood that the Yankees had to do "what was best for them," including financially. Whether it would be the best for the team remained to be seen. The Rivera-Wetteland combo had been a key part of the Yankees' 1996 season. Rivera said, "People said we were amazing. I guess we were."

After a preseason game, teammate Derek Jeter teased Rivera about his new role and his new clothes. "Now that you're a closer, you're all changed," Jeter said. The joke was that, even with some new and more expensive clothes, his higher salary, his new role, and a new baby boy, Rivera was entirely unchanged. By 1997, Rivera already called everyone "bro" and his teammates called him "Mo." He was unfailingly polite to clubhouse attendants and fans bearing gifts and showed no signs—nor would he ever—of developing the bigger-than-life ego associated with pitchers and especially with closers. His delivery was smooth; his philosophy was, "Just play baseball. Throw strikes." He added, though: "Go after hitters. When they're in the batter's box, they're the enemy. If you give them a chance, they'll kill you. Don't let them breathe. Never get beat with your second-best pitch. I learned that from Wetteland. Play hard. God gave me this talent, so I use it."

Rivera called the batter the "enemy," and sportswriter Buster Olney and others have said that Rivera strikes people out with "an assassin's cool efficiency," but he has never shown or reported feeling the anger that many other pitchers describe as necessary to give them their power and concentration. Throwing a pitch, Rivera would bare his teeth in concentration and, since childhood, he had hated to lose. At the same time, he thinks baseball is fun and has always said he would quit the day he found he was just playing the game for the paycheck. He loved being a Yankee and putting on the pinstripes and would sometimes come early to the stadium just to sit in the dugout and imagine what it was like when Mickey Mantle and Babe Ruth played there.

Rivera never forgot where he came from. He said he was like the other boys of his village. The combination of his upbringing—knowing how hard people worked, seeing how people took care of each other—and his belief that he just happened to have been given this gift helped him keep baseball in perspective. Baseball was never his whole life. By 1997, he and his wife, Clara, had two children, the three-year-old son who bore his name, and the new baby, Jafet. For much of the year, Clara was raising the boys in Panama, to be around their families. They wanted them to be Panamanian children and to go to school there and be raised in that culture. "Panama is home," Rivera said. He still missed it.

The Yankees went into the 1997 season not knowing if Rivera could play three days in a row, which he had not often done as the setup man. As a setup man, he would often pitch three innings in a game, rest for a day, then pitch again. The team could not afford to have him get tired and lose even a few miles per hour off his fastball. Yet the real question for a closer is if he can stand the pressure. Goose Gossage said, "You're standing on the mound at the end of the game, and you're either the hero or the goat. It's that simple. Can you come back from the nights you fail and start all over again?" That is not, Gossage said, a skill that can be taught. It is a matter of character. "That," says Rivera, "is what I like most about the job."

THE CUTTER

Rivera and the Yankees started 1997 off badly. Rivera blew three of his first six save situations. In mid-April, the team was tied for last place in the division. Yet when Rivera took the field on April 14, he was greeted by cheers from the crowd. The fans still trusted him.

Then, early in the season, Rivera developed a new tool to go along with his mental strength and focus. This was his cut fastball, a pitch so closely associated with his success as a pitcher that it is hard to remember that he did not have the pitch in 1995 or 1996.

Rivera was playing catch with a teammate, the pitcher Ramiro Mendoza. The day Rivera's fastball started to cut, he may or may not have been fiddling with it. (He has told the story both ways.) Either the ball just started sliding right and he did not know why, or else he was tinkering with his pitch. "I always like to play . . . with the grip of the baseball and see what it does. If it does something funny, I always pay attention to what it does and why." Rivera told one reporter that he had run his "fingers along the ball's seams and released it with extra pressure from his middle finger." Mendoza quickly tired of playing catch with Rivera that day: too many bruises where the ball bounced off him. When Rivera tried the pitch in a game a week later, the ball was still cutting left, much to the surprise of catcher Joe Girardi, whom Rivera didn't warn, and the hitters.

WHY RIVERA IS HARD TO HIT

The cut fastball has continued to bewilder most hitters (and sports commentators) since Rivera unleashed it. Broadcaster Jim Kaat said that it defied logic: "Hitters know it's coming in that one little box, and they still can't hit it."

For more than a decade, hitters have agreed. "You know what pitch you're getting from him, you get ready for that pitch, he throws you that pitch, and then your bat's breaking. It's no fun," said Johnny Damon, who hit against Rivera for the Red Sox before he joined the Yankees. It's what batter after batter has said about Rivera's pitch. Why, though, do batters find it so hard to hit? Rivera is not the first pitcher to throw a cutter or even a cut fastball. Al Leiter once threw a no-hitter with one, and Goose Gossage had one, too.

Johnny Damon of the Boston Red Sox broke his bat against Mariano Rivera during Game 2 of the 2004 American League Championship Series. Rivera's signature pitch, the cut fastball, breaks to the inside on left-handed batters, often causing their bats to break. Rivera developed the cut fastball during the 1997 season.

Much of Rivera's strength seems to be in his control of the pitch, for which he thanks pitching coach Mel Stottlemyre. Sandy Koufax said, "It's not what you throw, it's where you throw it." Rivera's cut fastball is a 94-to-97-mph (151-to-156-kph) pitch that looks even faster than it is (batters agree) and goes exactly where he wants it to go. A cutter is usually an off-speed pitch, but Rivera's is not. A cut fastball is often imperfectly controlled. Rivera's is not. Rivera can move the pitch up the strike zone little by little. As it moves up, it looks bigger, fooling batters into believing they can hit it. And his mental focus remains perfect: he thinks of nothing but the pitch he is throwing, sees nothing but the catcher's glove and any small changes in the batter's stance or position that warn him to adjust the pitch.

Rivera's cut fastball has been called "the single best pitch in the game" (Jim Thome), "the most dominant pitch of a generation" (Buster Olney) and, simply, "a buzzsaw" (the Braves' Chipper Jones). Chuck Knoblauch and others have joked that Rivera's cutter splinters so many bats that Louisville Slugger should pay him for the extra business he gives the company. The pitch cuts in sharply on the wrists of left-handed hitters, at the last minute. The batter cannot extend his arms and, even if the batter does make contact, he snaps his bat and his hit lacks power. Later Rivera was able to refine the cutter so it could break the other way as well. (He uses his index finger rather than his middle finger at the point of release).

In 1997, as a closer with his cut fastball, Rivera not only went to the All-Star Game but he also saved the game. By the end of the season, the Yankees were using him as the closer exclusively, but relief pitching would never again be as smooth as it had been when the Rivera-Wetteland team was in place.

BLOWN SAVE

The Yankees were expected to win the World Series that year. Instead they lost in the first round of play-offs to the

Cleveland Indians. Rivera's blown save in Game 4 was a large part of their defeat. Facing Sandy Alomar, Jr., Rivera gave up a home run, and the Yankees lost the game when they had been only four outs away from eliminating the Indians. They then lost Game 5 and the division series. That kind of failure has been enough to destroy young relievers, because they become afraid and tense up. Rivera denies that he has even given the loss much thought. This statement wasn't entirely true. He refused to watch video of the game for a month. But he then came up with his own explanation of what happened that night.

Buster Olney says that Rivera's self-confidence protects him. Rivera was able to see Alomar's home run as proof of his own power. If he had not been pitching, Rivera told himself, the ball would not have been thrown as hard and would not have gone out of the park: "The power in the home run had come from Rivera, the pitcher believed, and not from Alomar. Even in a moment that would have been a devastating failure for any other closer, Rivera believed he was in complete control." Alomar's home run did not make him doubt himself or his abilities. He would not give up another postseason home run for four years.

THE BEST YANKEE TEAM OF ALL TIME?

The 1998 Yankees were a determined team, coming out of that frustrating 1997 loss. Before the season started, general manager Bob Watson was replaced by Brian Cashman, who had been assistant general manager.

During spring training, George Steinbrenner asked Joe Torre if any team had ever finished the season 162–0. No, but the Yankees would finish the season having won 114 games. (Only the 1906 Cubs had done better, winning 116.) The Yankee franchise itself would list the 1998 team as one of the five best in history. The 1996 Yankees had talent and luck and they were hungry; the 1998 Yankees just dominated all season.

Mariano Rivera waved to Yankee fans during the victory parade to celebrate the team's 1998 World Series win. With Rivera were pitchers Mike Stanton *(left)* and Ramiro Mendoza. The 1998 Yankees, who had 114 regular-season wins, are considered among the best Yankee teams ever.

On May 17, David Wells pitched the thirteenth perfect game of the twentieth century: no runs, no hits, no walks. (On July 18, 1999, David Cone of the Yankees pitched another. The perfect games seemed further proof of the dominance of the two older pitchers and of continuing Yankee power.) In 1997, the team had struggled. In 1998, the *New York Post*'s George King wrote a May 24 article headlined, "The A.L. East Race Is Over!" This was, of course, an exaggeration. But when the Yankees clinched on August 29, the earliest of any team in the twentieth century, they did not even realize they had done it. Reporters figured it

☆ ☆ ☆ ☆ ☆
RIVERA AND HIS FAITH

During a game against the Braves on July 16, 1999, Mariano Rivera heard a voice say, "I am the one who has you here." Rivera understands this to be the voice of God. Rivera was already a man of deep faith. He wore a gold cross under his shirt, and he was part of a group of Yankees who read the Bible together before games.

Rivera began to think about what this message might mean for him. That December, he stood in a church in Panama, weeping from emotion, and said that he planned to play baseball for four more years and then would retire to become a minister. Although a team without Rivera was a frightening thought, Yankees general manager Brian Cashman said, "It sounds like he's got peace of mind, which is something many of us on this earth look for. For that, I'm happy for him." The four-year mark was not absolutely firm but, Rivera said, "I love the game, but I love God more."

Since that time, Rivera has contributed money toward building a church in his town in Panama. (Teammate David Cone said that only when speaking about that church did Rivera become out later that night. The team ended the season 22 games ahead of the second-place Red Sox.

As a closer, Rivera could never produce anything as rare and glamorous as a perfect game, but he produced Rivera magic. Although he missed 13 games early in the season with a strained groin, Rivera had an ERA of 1.91 in the 1998 regular season. Unlike most closers, who usually will just pitch the ninth inning, he would work two innings when necessary. He continued to refine his pitch. Teammates David Wells and Graeme Lloyd taught him that he could get an even better

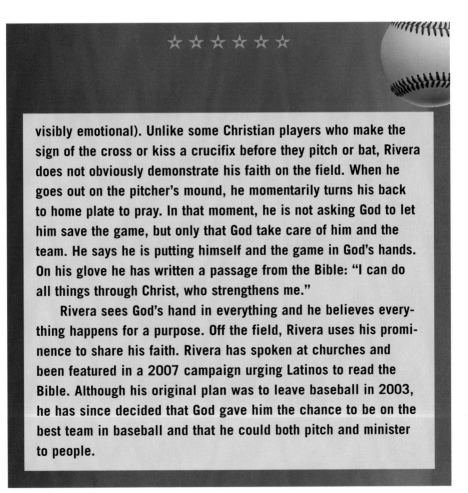

★ ★ ★ ★ ☆

visibly emotional). Unlike some Christian players who make the sign of the cross or kiss a crucifix before they pitch or bat, Rivera does not obviously demonstrate his faith on the field. When he goes out on the pitcher's mound, he momentarily turns his back to home plate to pray. In that moment, he is not asking God to let him save the game, but only that God take care of him and the team. He says he is putting himself and the game in God's hands. On his glove he has written a passage from the Bible: "I can do all things through Christ, who strengthens me."

Rivera sees God's hand in everything and he believes everything happens for a purpose. Off the field, Rivera uses his prominence to share his faith. Rivera has spoken at churches and been featured in a 2007 campaign urging Latinos to read the Bible. Although his original plan was to leave baseball in 2003, he has since decided that God gave him the chance to be on the best team in baseball and that he could both pitch and minister to people.

break on his cutter with a scuffed ball. "I never knew that," he said. "If I had a scuffed ball before, I'd throw it out. One day they played catch with me with two balls. One was scuffed, one wasn't. I saw the way the scuffed ball moved and said, 'Uh-oh. This is fun.'"

In the postseason, Rivera was six for six in save opportunities, and his ERA for all three rounds of the postseason was 0.00. As he recorded the last out of the World Series against the San Diego Padres, Rivera fell on the mound, raising his arms in the air. "I was thanking God for everything," he said later.

1999

The Yankees continued to be a team unified by tragedy, comradeship, and fantastic baseball. Darryl Strawberry was diagnosed with cancer in 1998. In 1999, Joe Torre was treated for prostate cancer. The fathers of several members of the team died during the season. The Yankees were a team that hugged and cried a lot, and the adversity made them close.

It was in 1999 that Metallica's "Enter Sandman" began to be used as Rivera's music in Yankee Stadium. At the stadium, a player coming onto the field has individual "theme" music. Most players choose their own, but "Enter Sandman" was chosen for Rivera, who does not listen to popular music and, in fact, did not even know what the song was until several years later. (He approved.) The lyrics speak of a kind of nightmare state in which you are "gripping your pillow tight"—a commentary on the experience that batters have when they face him. From July 8, 1999, to June 24, 2000, Rivera did not let a single inherited runner score. In 1999, he led the league in saves, save percentage, and relief ERA. What continued to make Rivera untouchable, aside from his cutter, was his concentration and his ability to put a loss behind him. "A closer needs a short memory," he says. After blowing three saves in five games in early July, he then saved the next 28 in a row, including six games in the postseason.

Yankees first baseman Tino Martinez (24) jumped into the arms of Mariano Rivera after the Yankees defeated the Mets in Game 5 to win the 2000 World Series. Among the others celebrating were catcher Jorge Posada and Scott Brosius (18). Rivera is the only pitcher to record the final out in three straight World Series.

RIVERA IN THE POSTSEASON

The Yankees breezed through the postseason in 1999—beating Texas in three games to win the American League Division Series and losing only one game to Boston to capture the American League Championship Series. The Yankees then swept Atlanta to win their second straight World Series. Rivera's postseason pitching was exceptional in 1999, even by

Rivera standards. His performance won him the World Series Most Valuable Player award—an honor that only two other relief pitchers (Oakland's Rollie Fingers and the Yankees' John Wetteland) had ever received. He had thrown 12 1/3 scoreless innings in eight postseason appearances. He had converted all six of his save opportunities. Rivera also won the Rolaids Relief Man of the Year. On November 4, the government of Panama awarded him the Manuel Amador Guerrero Order, one of Panama's highest honors.

A year later, in the 2000 postseason, Rivera had a bad moment on the mound. In 1995, he had stood in Seattle's Kingdome and struck out Mike Blowers. In 2000, during the American League Championship Series, in the Mariners' new Safeco Field, Mariners second baseman Mark McLemore hit a groundball off Rivera, scoring two runs, one of which was charged against him. It was the first postseason run he had given up in more than three years. Rivera just said, "We won the game. Who cares about streaks?"

The Yankees went to the World Series again, this time against the Mets—the first Subway Series since 1956, when the Yankees had beaten the Brooklyn Dodgers. Rivera saved the fourth and fifth games of the Series. Game 5 ended with a long hit by Mike Piazza that was caught by Bernie Williams just short of the warning track. The Yankees had won the Series. Rivera lifted his hands to the sky and screamed with joy. "I tell you what," he said. "It's the best feeling. Ever. And I've been there three times already."

Rivera had become the only pitcher ever to record the final out in three consecutive World Series.

"The most crucial factor and the greatest reason the Yankees are three-time champions is Rivera. He is the infallible weapon that no other teams have," wrote Jack Curry of the *New York Times*. Manager Joe Torre, coach Don Zimmer, numerous teammates, and members of other teams have said the same thing in different words, over and over again.

The Year
They Lost: 2001

By 2001, the Yankees had won the World Series three years in a row and four years out of the last five. They had won 16 of their last 17 World Series games. Anyone who had ever hated the Yankees, with their dynasties (this one was now being compared to that of the 1950s) and their big budget, hated them again.

The players who had been on the '96 team and those who came later expected to win. The 1996 win had been a joy, as rookies and old-timers celebrated a wonderful victory. They had been glad after the 2000 win, of course, but by this time they were just doing what was expected of them. Nothing else was acceptable, to George Steinbrenner, to the players themselves, or to the fans and the press, who could be merciless. In 1999 and 2000, Gold Glove second baseman Chuck

Knoblauch developed a throwing problem for psychological reasons no one was able to understand. When Knoblauch became unable to make the simplest throw to first, he was booed and razzed until Derek Jeter requested that the fans stop harassing him. (They did.)

The expectation for the Yankees was that they would win every game and be in first place in the division at all times. The Yankees felt that way themselves at times, except that most seasoned players knew that everyone has an "off" day. (Paul O'Neill, who seemed to think that he had to maintain a 1.000 batting average, nearly drove himself crazy, demolishing water coolers and throwing helmets in frustration.)

No one booed Mariano. A Rivera loss continued to be unusual and nearly unthinkable. People didn't boo—they were too shocked. "New York demands a lot," Rivera said several years later. "If you don't do your job, there are questions. You've been spoiled." The "you" in the last sentence referred to the press and the fans, Rivera said.

CONTRACT MATTERS

During the off-season, Rivera was in negotiations with the Yankees over his salary. Rivera's salary was often in arbitration. A player and a team may go to arbitration if they cannot agree on contract terms. Under arbitration, the player and the club submit salary figures to an arbitrator, who picks one or the other. In 1999, Rivera won his arbitration case, winning a salary of $4.25 million. In 2000, he lost. That season, he was paid $7.25 million, not the $9.25 million he had sought. His arbitration loss was reported to him while he was working out. Still doing sit-ups, he said, "O.K., thank you." When reporters solemnly asked him about the matter, he just laughed. "It's like somebody died in here. I'm not upset at all, and I have to concentrate on what I have to do this year." In 2001, his contract appeared headed to arbitration again. But with a new agent, Fernando Cuza, negotiations were renewed, and Rivera

Mariano Rivera stretched his hamstring during warm-ups on February 16, 2001, at the Yankees' spring-training facility in Tampa, Florida. On that day, the Yankees and Rivera agreed to a four-year, $39.99 million contract—the highest ever for a closer at that time.

received a four-year, $39.99 million contract. The deal made him the highest-paid closer in baseball.

PANAMA IS HOME

In August 1998, Rafael Hermoso of the *Daily News* had quoted Rivera as saying, "I won't trade Panama for New York." By the end of each season, Rivera said, he started to miss Panama and the tranquillity of his town. "It's my land."

Rivera tried to maintain his Panamanian life and his American life. He had a beautiful house in Panama, in his hometown. It was a mansion by local standards, with two stories, elegant columns, and a swimming pool. To people in his town, it stood as a symbol of his great success. For years in the United States, he had maintained only a small apartment in New Rochelle, in Westchester County, north of the Bronx.

Although he had urged his father to take it easy, Captain Rivera continued to go out on the fishing boat. Rivera's parents were still living in the house in which he was raised, although it had been updated and made more comfortable. And Rivera was always active in the community, sending baseball equipment to the children and giving them toys at Christmas. On Mother's Day, which is on December 8 in Panama, he would hold a party and give large appliances and furniture to women in the town. He also donated many thousands of dollars worth of medical equipment to a local hospital. Although he would give presents, most often he would try to give in ways that help people help themselves. Later he would build computer centers for children in Panama so that they could grow up and find better jobs, and he became involved with the fishermen's co-op, giving the fisherman nets that allowed them to fulfill new regulations concerning the size of fish they were allowed to catch. When he built his house in Panama, he used local labor, ensuring that the money he was paying would go to people in his community.

Rivera was dealing well with the problems that may arise when a member of a relatively poor family becomes rich: how does he contribute toward his family and his community without making them his dependents? His father's refusal to give up his work until he was of normal retirement age suggests that the Rivera family did not want to live off their son's earnings. His activities received little publicity in the United States, but before the 2003 season began, Rivera was awarded the "Thurman Munson Award," given by the Association for the Help of Retarded Children for his charity work.

THE MOVE TO THE U.S.

Right after the 2000 season, Rivera moved his family to Westchester County, New York. After the move, the family would spend about a month in Panama each year, to be there at Christmas. The *New York Times* reported that Rivera feared that his income put his family at risk for kidnappers. Although Panama did not have a high rate of kidnapping, the neighboring country of Colombia did. A Colombian guerrilla group involved in drug trafficking was behind most of the kidnappings, and it had started to move into Panama. (Four years later, the mother of Detroit Tigers reliever Ugueth Urbina was kidnapped from Venezuela and held for ransom in Colombia for six months.) Rivera had not wanted to move his family, but "for safety, I have to look out for my kids and my family. . . . All it takes is one crazy maniac guy who wakes up that morning with my name in their mind, and I can't tolerate that."

9/11

On September 11, 2001, Muslim extremists flew commercial jets into the World Trade Center in New York City and the Pentagon near Washington, D.C. A fourth hijacked jet crashed in a field in Pennsylvania. Normal life in New York City was suspended as clouds of ash blanketed parts of the city and the acrid smell of smoldering buildings and burnt plastic drifted more than 100 blocks north of the collapsed World Trade Center. Makeshift memorials were created at city firehouses and at Union Square Park on 14th Street. Every streetlight was plastered with homemade signs and pictures of people who were missing. New Yorkers broke all ordinary rules of New York etiquette. In grocery stores, restaurants, and Laundromats, strangers took one another's hands and asked, "Are you all right? Is your family all right?" before conducting any ordinary business. It was a city dazed, shocked, and dizzy with confusion and grief.

New York sports teams, including the Yankees, who were still playing the regular season, struggled to understand what had happened. They were not New Yorkers by birth, and few even maintained apartments in the city, although Chuck Knoblauch and Tino Martinez could see the World Trade Center from their windows and Derek Jeter lived only a little farther uptown.

Mariano Rivera said, "I am not from the U.S. I still feel like some part of me came down when those buildings came down. There were tears coming out of my eyes. It was a different feeling than I ever had." Only two days before September 11, he and his wife had been driving on the New Jersey side of the Hudson River, and he had admired the towers shining in the night.

Major-league play was suspended for six days. It was the first time since World War I that any event but a league strike had caused play to be suspended. Four days after the attacks, many Yankees met for the first time and knelt together in the field at Yankee Stadium. The flags above the frieze—the white fence-like structure high above the outfield bleachers—hung at half-mast.

The various New York sports teams found ways to help the city recover. Some Yankees went to the Lexington Avenue armory, where people were bringing DNA samples of missing family members in the hopes that body parts found in the rubble could be identified. The Yankees who went there were confused, at first, about their role. Were they intruding on people's grief? What were they doing there? They came to understand that they were indeed welcome and that their presence there could, briefly, cheer people up. Bernie Williams said to a woman who had lost her husband, "I'm not a doctor, I'm not a counselor, I don't know what to say. All I know is, I think you need a hug." The players hugged people, signed autographs, posed for photographs, and shook hands. Yankee players also went to firehouses and to Ground Zero, the site of the fallen Twin Towers. Cell phones were pressed into their hands, with requests that they speak to the families of people who had died. Their presence brought relief.

THE BASEBALL SEASON RESUMES

On September 17, the resumption of the baseball season would serve the same function. Paul O'Neill said that it was almost as if the city needed something to get away from the tragedy, for a few hours at a time. Baseball is just a game, but it was part of normal life, and in the middle of a time of great uncertainty and pain, baseball was a reminder that life would go on. It would not go on in quite the same way. A tattered American flag found at Ground Zero hung above Yankee Stadium for the rest of the year. There was an enormous presence at the stadium of servicemen and servicewomen, firefighters, and police officers. Some were there to ensure security, others to be honored for their service to the city. Fans held up signs that said, "USA Fears Nobody/Play Ball" and "United We Stand/Special thanks to the FDNY-NYPD and all of the armed forces." The singing of "God Bless America" and "America the Beautiful" became new traditions.

The Yankees rapidly discovered that they were now the symbols of New York, for New Yorkers and for people across the country. Scott Brosius said that it was "amazing to see the transformation, because for the rest of that year we weren't the hated Yankees." Playing in Chicago on September 18, the Yankees saw signs that said things like "I love New York and even the Yankees"—not the usual reaction from White Sox fans. Yet the players were also residents of a country that had been attacked, and they suffered the same fears that others did. Flying into Chicago in a storm that shook their plane, Shane Spencer saw Chicago's famous Sears Tower and wondered if it would become a terrorist target, too.

The Yankees finished the regular season with 95 wins to capture the American League East. Two contradictory

Chicago White Sox fans at Comiskey Park showed their support for New York in a game played seven days after the September 11, 2001, terrorist attacks. The Yankees, instead of being the hated team of the past, became a symbol of New York for all of the United States.

theories were posed regarding the outcome of the postseason. One was the sense of "destiny" that the Yankees would win the World Series again, because they always won or because New York needed them to win or because there was a "mystique" about Yankee Stadium. ("Mystique and Aura, those are dancers at a nightclub, not things we concern ourselves with on the ball field," scoffed the Diamondbacks' star pitcher Curt Schilling.) The other was that the team had an extraordinary number of players who were injured or old or both. They had not had a strong season, they were not playing especially well, and it would not have been surprising if the Seattle Mariners with their 116 regular-season wins and their new Japanese star, Ichiro Suzuki, beat them handily.

Baseball was being played in an unusual atmosphere, for fans and for players. Shane Spencer said later:

> We didn't play our best ball. But still there was something magical. We had to go through some tough times. You come to the field and you want to play baseball. And they're having a special ceremony for the firefighters, and you're out there holding hands with firefighters and policemen, and they're all crying. And then you're crying. And the fans are crying. And you're looking at the people crying in the stands, and you're like, 'Is this really important?' But to the fans, it was. And we rode that. We just had some magical moments.

THE DIVISION SERIES AGAINST OAKLAND

Two of the magical moments against Oakland would be Jeter's defensive moves, a couple of plays that show up regularly on Yankees highlights. In Oakland, having lost the first two games at home, the Yankees faced elimination in the third. In Game 3, the A's were down 1-0 in the seventh inning, with Jeremy Giambi as the tying run on first. Terrence Long hit a ball to far right field. The ball bounced down the right-field line as Giambi headed to third; the third-base coach waved

Mayor Rudolph Giuliani of New York City congratulated Mariano Rivera after the Yankees defeated the Oakland A's in Game 5 to win the 2001 American League Division Series. Rivera had two saves and an ERA of 0.00 in the division series.

him home. Shane Spencer's throw missed both cutoff men, and then Jeter just appeared (it seemed) on the right side of the diamond to shovel the ball to catcher Jorge Posada in time to tag out Giambi. The out at home did more than just protect the Yankees' lead—it seemed to show that their weird magic was still at work and that, if Jeter needed to be somewhere a shortstop never was, he would be there. In the last game of the division series, at home, he would make a catch that took him backward and upside down into the front-row seats past third base. He emerged with his face bleeding, with bruises that would bother him for the rest of the season, but he was still holding the ball.

Rivera pitched five innings in the three games that the Yankees won, for an ERA of 0.00 and two saves. As he closed out the last inning, he leaped into the air, spinning a full 360 degrees with excitement.

THE CHAMPIONSHIP SERIES AGAINST SEATTLE

The Seattle Mariners' 116 regular-season wins had tied the all-time record, but they came to Yankee Stadium having lost the first two games of the American League Championship Series at home. Seattle was able to take Game 3, 14-3, but faltered in the next two games. Strong Yankee pitching continued to be a big part of Seattle's losses. Rivera pitched in four games for one win and two saves. He had an ERA of 1.93, having let one run score against him. When the Mariners went down, 12-3, in the fifth game to lose the series, Yankee fans—no more polite than they ever were—jeered the Mariners and yelled, "Over-rated! Overrated!" Their manager, Lou Piniella, found himself thinking, "Boy, this city has suffered a lot, and tonight they let out a lot of emotions. I felt good for them, I really did—and that's a strange thought to come from a manager who's getting his ass kicked."

THE WORLD SERIES AGAINST ARIZONA

The Diamondbacks, the National League champions, felt bad for New York, of course, but not for the Yankees. They were a young franchise, but as a team they were, said Mark Grace, a "bunch of crotchety old guys who had never been to a World Series." For the first two games, played in Phoenix, it seemed that the Diamondbacks would win, easily. The pitching of Curt Schilling and Randy Johnson was overpowering as Arizona defeated New York 9-1 in the first game and 4-0 in the second game.

Back at Yankee Stadium, bomb dogs sniffed through the players' lockers and President George W. Bush threw out the first ball wearing a FDNY (Fire Department of New York) jacket. The Yankees' Roger Clemens won the first game at home, turning a 2-1 lead over to Rivera for the save.

Game 4 was one of those games that goes down in baseball history as too much like a movie to be real. Curt Schilling allowed only three hits and one run in the first seven innings, and at nearly midnight, the score was 3-1 in favor of Arizona.

☆ ☆ ☆ ☆ ☆

WHAT A SAVE IS

One of the most important statistics for a closer is number of saves. Rivera is third on the all-time career list, with 443 as of the end of the 2007 season. But what is a save? Most simply, it means a relief performance that preserves a lead. Officially, to be awarded a save, the closing pitcher must fulfill three requirements:

1. He must finish the game won by his team.
2. He does not receive the win (if a closer were brought in when his team was behind and the team rallied and won the game, he would be awarded a win, not a save.)
3. And (one of the following three conditions): He enters the game with a lead of no more than three runs and pitches at least one inning *or* he enters the game with the tying run on base, at bat, or on deck *or* he pitches effectively for at least three innings.

The save was made an official statistic in 1969, to reflect the growing importance of relief pitching, but the term was first used by a Chicago sportswriter, Jerome Holtzman, back in the 1950s.

It looked as if it was all over, except that the intangibles—Mystique? Yankee Stadium gremlins?—were still there. The wind blew Yankee balls foul that otherwise would have been caught. Experienced Diamondback players bumped into one another making routine plays. Still, Byung-Hyun Kim came in to close and struck out three in the eighth inning. Then, in the ninth, Paul O'Neill singled—it was his last season in baseball and he could just about limp to first base—and Tino Martinez's first hit of the Series was a home run that tied the game. In the bottom of the tenth inning, Jeter came to bat. It was October 31, and there was a full moon over the stadium. With two outs, a full count, and the bells tolling midnight, Jeter hit a home run to win the game and the stadium went screamingly wild, shaking so hard it felt as if the whole place might fall down. A Yankee fan promptly held up a sign that read "Mr. November."

The Yankees and the Diamondbacks were now playing November baseball. Game 5 began with the release of a tame American golden eagle, which flew around and then returned to its handler. Baseball continued to be, as one commentator had said, "a beacon of hope" for a city full of grief and despair. But Game 5 did not encourage hope, as the Yankees again were losing in the ninth inning—this time by a score of 2-0. The Yankees just were not hitting. They had not been hitting throughout the Series. Then, in the bottom of the ninth, with Byung-Hyun Kim closing, with two outs and a runner on base, third baseman Scott Brosius came to the plate and hit a home run. Kim fell to his knees in agony. In the twelfth inning, rookie Alfonso Soriano's single brought Chuck Knoblauch home for the winning run. Curt Schilling, asked again about Yankee mystique and aura, said, "I didn't know they'd make an appearance in Yankee Stadium." It was, said a fan's sign, "A Yankee Miracle." "It's *Groundhog Day*," Joe Torre said. "I don't know what's going on."

Then the Series went back to Arizona, away from Yankee Stadium and the New York fans. But it wasn't a lack of magic that resulted in the Yankees' 15-2 loss in Game 6. Andy Pettitte was tipping his pitches—showing by his body language what he was going to throw—a habit he had been cured of, most of the time. The Series was tied and would be decided in Game 7. It would be the first World Series Game 7 that this Yankee dynasty had had to play.

GAME 7

New York was in the middle of an anthrax scare—the deadly virus had been found in City Hall and it seemed likely that another terrorist attack was in progress. (Letters containing anthrax were sent to various media outlets and U.S. Senate offices. The case has not yet been solved, although no letters have been sent since November 2001.) A newly uneasy New York watched Game 7 on big-screen TVs in Rockefeller Center and in Times Square.

Game 7 was going to be the close of an era, no matter how the game ended. Paul O'Neill, a Yankee for nine years, was retiring, and so was Scott Brosius. Chuck Knoblauch would be traded, still unable to solve the problem that left him throwing wildly. Luis Sojo would soon be gone, and so would Tino Martinez. Players like David Cone and Joe Girardi were already on other teams.

Before the game, Joe Torre had asked Yankee trainer Gene Monahan to speak to the players. Monahan, a Yankee trainer for 29 years, spoke movingly about the team's history, and about the players' pride and their hard work. He said that he knew that all the players would do their best, handle themselves with dignity and professionalism, and help one another out. He knew, he said, "you're going to walk off as champions." It was, one player said later, a perfect speech. Then, as the players wiped their eyes, applauded, and got ready to leave, Rivera did something entirely uncharacteristic. He got up in the meeting and spoke. Rivera was considered a team leader, but by example, not through making speeches.

Rivera made the team a promise: "We are going to win tonight. . . . Just get the ball to me, and we will win." He said: "Whatever happens tonight is in the hands of God." Being an athlete, as well as a Christian, he finished: "Let's kick some butt."

Teammates who knew him well found it an odd, uncharacteristic, and disquieting speech. Although many of his teammates were also practicing Christians, they were less comforted than Rivera by the idea that the game was in God's hands. Still, having the game in Rivera's hands seemed safe enough. He had not blown a postseason lead in 1,490 days.

THE END OF THE GAME

The pitchers were Schilling and Clemens, and the game went into the eighth inning tied 1-1. Bench coach Don Zimmer told Torre to put in Rivera, but Torre said he would wait until they had a lead. Just have Soriano hit a home run, he said, and that would solve the whole problem. Then, on an 0-2 pitch, Soriano hit a home run. Problem solved. Torre put in Rivera.

An announcer said, "So many teams have tried, so many teams have failed against Mariano Rivera." Since 1998, he had gone 23 for 23 in postseason save opportunities. His ERA for World Series play was 0.70, the lowest in history. He was the only pitcher to have recorded the final out in three consecutive World Series. Mike Lupica of the New York *Daily News* had called Rivera "the greatest clutch athlete in history." In 2001, Rivera had a career-high 50 saves in the regular season.

In the eighth inning, Rivera struck out the side. Major-league officials gave the Fox network the go-ahead to set up the World Series trophy presentation stage in the Yankees clubhouse: Rivera was hot and needed only three more outs. The game was over.

THE BOTTOM OF THE NINTH

At exactly 9:11 P.M. (a bit of timing that fans found ominous), Rivera allowed a single to the leadoff batter, 37-year-old Mark Grace. Arizona put in a pinch runner, David Dellucci, for Grace.

Damian Miller bunted—and it's not easy to bunt against Rivera. The ball bounced twice, and Rivera threw it to second for the force out. Rivera had committed *one* error in 455 major-league games. He now committed his second: He did not get a good grip on the ball and he overthrew second base. Derek Jeter, covering second, stretched out his arm to try to catch the ball and was spiked by the sliding runner.

Men on first and second; no outs.

Jay Bell then bunted toward Rivera, who fielded the ball cleanly and threw it to Brosius on third. Brosius caught it, but rather than throwing to first or second for the double play, he held the ball. There was one out, but there should have been two.

Shortstop Tony Womack hit a broken-bat double. The score was 2-2, with Womack on second and Bell on third.

Rivera then hit batter Craig Counsell on the wrist, and the bases were loaded for Luis Gonzalez, Arizona's best hitter.

The Yankee infield gathered on the mound to decide where to position themselves. They decided to play the infield in: extra-base hits didn't matter now, all that mattered was getting Bell out before he could score from third. It was a reasonable decision. If batters hit Rivera at all, they usually get ground-outs (102 in the 2001 season) or pop-ups (53 in 2001). Still, Gonzalez was a fly-ball hitter. After the Yankees positioned themselves, Fox announcer Tim McCarver said, "Left-handers get a lot of broken-bat hits into the shallow part of the outfield. That's the danger of bringing the infield in with a guy like Rivera on the mound."

Gonzalez choked up on his bat to give it more speed. He stepped back slightly to give himself more room to hit a ball

Arizona Diamondbacks left fielder Luis Gonzalez hit a bases-loaded single off Mariano Rivera in the bottom of the ninth inning in Game 7 of the 2001 World Series. The resulting run gave Arizona the victory over the Yankees in the Series.

that breaks on the inside. He fouled off the first pitch. The second, a nearly perfect Rivera pitch on the batter's hands, he hit, breaking his bat, but the ball flew over the heads of the infielders. It landed in the grass to the left of second base, a place Jeter would have been able to cover if the infield was not playing in. The Diamondbacks had just won their first World Series, and Rivera had just lost his first—for himself and for the team.

WHAT HAD HAPPENED

The Yankees had done their best, keeping baseball going into the month of November. An injured team, hitting terribly (.183 as a team in the World Series, with only 14 runs in 7 games), had given the city some extra weeks of distraction. But what had gone wrong in the bottom of the ninth?

The theories are many. Brosius's failure to turn the double play was costly. A *New York Times* headline said, "Rivera Places the Blame in Brosius' Hand." Brosius thought this was unfair—and extremely unlike Rivera, who never blamed a teammate— but all Rivera had said was that he thought they might have gotten the double play. Torre, first baseman Tino Martinez, and everyone else agreed.

Buster Olney wrote that Rivera was tired. His pitch speed was down from 95 or 96 miles per hour (153 or 154 kilometers per hour) in the eighth inning to 93 or 94 miles per hour (150 or 151 kilometers per hour) in the ninth. He said that Rivera's throwing error to second was caused by the Arizona ballpark's unique strip of dirt between the mound and home plate, and that the ball bounced oddly, as Buck Showalter had meant it to do, and so Rivera didn't get it firmly.

Dave Anderson of the *New York Times* had written back on October 7 that Rivera's sore ankle was making him more hittable. He had blown seven save opportunities. He had worked extra innings.

Charles Euchner, author of *The Last Nine Innings,* says that the Diamondbacks had a strategy, designed by Mike Rizzo, their director of scouting. Since Rivera's cutter breaks in on the hands of left-handers, they should step back, giving themselves room to swing. Usually if players do this, Rivera simply throws to another part of the strike zone, but it is what the Arizona players say they did.

Several fans say that when TV cameras showed Rivera in the dugout between the eighth and ninth innings, he looked uncharacteristically ill with tension.

Rivera had little to say at the time about the loss. As the Diamondbacks rejoiced, Rivera walked quietly off the field, looking much as he always did after an inning. He ignored Martinez, who tried to put an arm around him, and walked into the dugout and toward the clubhouse.

Reporters, incredulous, asked Rivera over and over again what had happened, and in English and Spanish, he answered them politely. He looked, said Jack Curry, "weary and sweaty," but calm. He said quietly:

> I tell you what: it's hard. But we did everything. We gave everything we had and, you know, I just didn't find a way to win it. We did everything. We left everything on the field and they beat us. . . . I don't have nothing on my mind about the future. I'm not going to second-guess myself either. I'm feeling good. I just couldn't finish it out. I threw the pitches I wanted to throw and they hit it. . . . We went through a good season. . . . I'm not going to go back and say, "Oh, we should have won." This is what happened.

Not even Steinbrenner, whom Rivera calls "Mr. George," blamed his closer. Steinbrenner blamed the TV crews for setting up the celebration after the eighth inning: it gave them bad luck.

Rivera's final conclusions—at least the ones he was willing to share with the public—came a little later. If the Yankees had won the Series, Rivera's teammate Enrique Wilson would have been on American Airlines Flight 587 on November 12, going home to the Dominican Republic. With the victory parade canceled, Wilson changed his reservation and went home earlier. The plane he would have been on crashed in Queens, New York, killing everyone on board. Rivera told Wilson, "I'm glad we lost the World Series, because it means I still have a friend." Rivera had been wrong about the win, but he believed he was right about the outcome of the game being in God's hands.

Rivera's other conclusion reminds us again why, aside from good health, he has remained dominant as a closer for so long: Although he hates to lose, he isn't afraid of failure. He *wants* the responsibility of having the game depend on him and—as long as he feels he has done his job and placed his pitches—he is willing to accept the outcome. "I know I'm going to save the game or I'm gonna lose it. I love it."

Despite his loss in the last game of the 2001 World Series, Rivera again won the Rolaids Relief Man of the Year Award for the best performance by a relief pitcher that season. Relief pitchers have been called "firemen" because they go into a hot situation and put out the "fire" of the other team's rally. The trophy is a gold-plated fireman's helmet. At the ceremony in which Rivera received his award, he presented it to the Fire Department of New York, for its actions on and after September 11. He said, "I want to present this trophy to the true saviors, the true closers. I think the rescue department of New York City deserves this honor. They were an inspiration for us to continue this season."

"Not the Same Team": 2002–2006

In July 2002, Mariano Rivera gave up a grand slam against Cleveland that lost the game for the Yankees. A few days later, he gave up a two-run single and was removed from the game with tightness in his right shoulder. "They don't think I have blood," he said. "They think I have oil, like a machine or something. Or batteries. Well, batteries die." At the same time, Rivera assured everyone that he was fine, that there was nothing for anyone to worry about. But three times in the 2002 season, Rivera was on the 15-day disabled list. Rivera would appear in only 45 games that season, the first time since 1998 that he had appeared in fewer than 61. Dueling headlines said, "Rivera No Longer Mr. Automatic" and "'Nuf Said: Mo Trusts His Stuff." "It's amazing when they hit a hit off me and a lot of friends call me and tell me, 'What's going on with me?'

because they get a hit," Rivera said. "I am still the same Mo." He recorded the 225th save of his career, surpassing the mark of 224 by Dave Righetti and making Rivera the Yankees' all-time save leader.

LOSSES

The Yankees of 2002 were not the Yankees of the dynasty any longer. Paul O'Neill, Scott Brosius, Tino Martinez, and Chuck Knoblauch retired or went to other teams after 2001. Rivera had lost some old friends and teammates, but an even more difficult loss came when his cousin Rubén Rivera was released from the team in March for stealing a glove and a bat belonging to Derek Jeter and selling them to a memorabilia dealer. He said he needed the money—major-league players begin to draw their salaries on April 15 and evidently his spring-training pay was not enough—but, as Bernie Williams said, he could have borrowed the money. Rubén had been on the verge of taking over Gerald Williams's place as the backup center fielder.

Mariano said little publicly about the theft. "I want you guys to give me some respect," he told reporters. "I am disappointed and prefer not to say anything." A friend said that Mariano was "devastated." He had urged the Yankees to re-sign his cousin, whose career had foundered after the Yankees traded him in 1997 to the San Diego Padres. Rubén Rivera had been considered the more talented of the Rivera cousins—in 1995 the Yankees believed Rubén was the next Mickey Mantle—and had contributed to the 1996 World Series win. Rubén, however, had long been seen as undisciplined and immature, on the field and in his personal life. He had, perhaps, all of Mariano's physical talent but not his "strong mind."

Although the Yankees won the American League East in 2002, the Anaheim Angels eliminated them easily in the American League Division Series. Jorge Posada said, "It looked like they wanted it more than we did." Rather than coming back from deficits and rallying in late innings, the Yankees seemed to give up when they were not winning. When a reporter spoke to Jeter of how much the team had accomplished in past years, Jeter said, "*Some* of us have."

"THE STRENGTH OF GOD"

On November 20, the Riveras' third son was born. His name, Jaziel, means "the strength of God." Although Mariano and Clara Rivera had planned to give the boy this name, it came to have extra significance for them. After the baby's birth, by Caesarean section (the baby was big and Mrs. Rivera is small), Clara Rivera began to bleed so heavily that her doctor feared that her life was in danger. Instead, she recovered quickly and was able to leave the hospital after only a few days.

Rivera's faith in God was strengthened even more by this experience. That spring, Pastor Jim Cymbala of the Brooklyn Tabernacle, which was the church of Clara's doctor, asked Rivera to speak to the congregation about his life and his faith. Rivera spoke freely about his childhood poverty and about how his faith had helped him in difficult times. Earlier, a few weeks after Clara was released from the hospital, the Riveras had given a party at their house for about 20 members of the hospital staff, to say thank you for the good care they had taken of Clara and Jaziel. Because it was raining, Rivera parked the guests' cars so that they would not get wet. Since his earliest days in the clubhouse, his courtesy and his gratitude to others characterized his interactions, and it was a courtesy he extended automatically not just to team managers or hospital doctors but to people who worked hard for less money and prestige.

2003

Rivera had a career-low ERA of 1.66 for the 2003 season. He could still save games (40 of them, plus five wins), but he could not save the team. In the years since their last World Series

Mariano Rivera's teammates surrounded him after the Yankees beat the Boston Red Sox in the eleventh inning of Game 7 of the 2003 American League Championship Series. Rivera pitched the ninth, tenth, and eleventh innings of that game— the longest he had pitched in one game since 1996. He was named the Most Valuable Player of the championship series.

win, Yankees owner George Steinbrenner had gone back to his practice of packing the team with superstars, responding to losses by signing yet another high-priced player. The team signed Alex Rodriguez, Jason Giambi, and Gary Sheffield, among others, while it would soon trade the young Alfonso Soriano who, in both the 2002 and 2003 seasons, had accumulated more than 30 home runs and 30 steals. Soriano was the kind of player who had made up the 1996 team, but now Steinbrenner would not wait for a talented young player to mature. *The Onion*, a weekly satirical newspaper made up of fake stories, published an article headlined, "Yankees Ensure 2003 Pennant by Signing Every Player in Baseball." In 2003, it seemed as if this strategy of signing big-name players—which failed in the 1980s—might be working for Steinbrenner, as the team won 101 games in the regular season and then beat Minnesota in the American League Division Series.

In the final game of the American League Championship Series, Rivera pitched three innings against Boston—innings 9 through 11—and shut the Red Sox out. It was the most innings Rivera had pitched in a game since 1996. As Aaron Boone hit a home run to win it in the eleventh inning, Rivera ran out of the dugout and fell to his knees in joy. "I didn't even think. I just went to the mound and hugged the mound," he said later. With 1 win, 2 saves, and a 1.12 ERA, Rivera won the MVP award for the American League Championship Series. His lifetime postseason ERA was down to an amazing 0.75. Rivera remained steady through both slumps and awards. "You just want to go in there and pitch," he would say. As his numbers had risen through years of steady play, more people spoke of Rivera as a future Hall of Famer.

The Yankees faced the Florida Marlins in the World Series—Rivera's sixth World Series appearance—and they were favored to win. Rivera posted an ERA of 0.00 for the Series, but the Yankees lost in six games. Playing with eagerness and joy, the Marlins, a team of young players mixed with old stars, resembled the Yankees of 1996, not the Yankees of 2003.

2004

Boston Red Sox fans remember 2004 as the year that their team finally won a World Series and put to rest "The Curse of the Bambino," which, legend says, was brought on by the team's sale of Babe Ruth to the Yankees after the 1919 season. Yankee fans remember 2004 as the year in which their traditional rivals won the World Series and they lost, horribly.

The Yankees again won 101 regular-season games in 2004. They had stars, but the team was not the cohesive unit it had been. Alex Rodriguez, the most expensive baseball player in history, was learning to play third base and was inclined to compete with Jeter. Aaron Boone had destroyed his knee playing basketball in the off-season. When the star-packed team lost 22-0 to the Cleveland Indians on August 31, it was the worst defeat a Yankee team had ever suffered. Still, the Yankees won the American League East and the American League Division Series against the Minnesota Twins. Rivera's 53 saves were a career high, and he won the Rolaids Relief Man of the Year Award for the third time.

THE MOST TERRIBLE LOSS

In Game 1 of the American League Championship Series against Boston, played at Yankee Stadium, two dramas unfolded at the same time. The less important one was that Yankee Mike Mussina pitched six perfect innings, only to have the Yankees' 8-0 lead dwindle to 8-7 in the eighth inning. If the Yankees had lost, it would have equaled the biggest blown lead in postseason history.

The more important drama was the wait to see if Mariano Rivera would be available to close—or if he would be in the stadium at all.

Three days earlier, during the celebration of the division series victory, Clara Rivera had come to tell Mariano that there had been a family tragedy. Her cousin Victor Dario Avila and his 14-year-old son, also named Victor, had died in an accident in the swimming pool at the Riveras' house in Panama. Avila had been a childhood friend of Rivera's, and the boy was, he told teammate Luis Sojo, like another son to him. Avila worked as a cook on a fishing boat and was also a gardener at the Riveras' house. While Avila was working, the boy, nicknamed Leo, jumped into the pool but pulled a live electric wire into the water with him, perhaps by tripping over it. His father dove in to rescue him and also died. The electric wire had been rigged by the house caretakers, also members of the Riveras' extended family, to keep the dogs out of the pool.

Mariano and Clara Rivera flew immediately to Panama, and no one knew when Mariano would be able to return or if he would be able to pitch when he did come back. In Panama, Rivera was hounded by the press, as local and U.S. reporters camped outside his house. The interest was, of course, a combination of genuine sympathy for a well-liked person and the sort of ghoulish fascination that tragedy—especially tragedy involving a famous person and a dead child—always attracts. After a photographer jumped on the roof of his SUV to take a picture of Rivera's pool and his house over the privacy wall, Rivera's mother came out to protest. Rivera then agreed that he would come out and answer questions and be photographed in exchange for the press leaving him and his family to mourn in private.

RIVERA'S ON THE WAY

When Rivera said he would come back and pitch on the day of the funeral, the Yankees sent a private jet for him. Fans followed his progress, cheering when the announcement was made that his plane had landed and that he was on his way to the stadium. When Rivera arrived, it still seemed that he would not be needed to close out the game, but then the Red Sox began to come back from their 8-0 deficit. Fans cheered again when he appeared in the bullpen to warm up, surely a combination of relief that Rivera was there to save the win and support for his willingness to come to the rescue at that moment. Fans nearly drowned out his theme song, "Enter Sandman," as he took the mound in the eighth inning, standing and cheering. It was a moment when Rivera's importance to the team and to the fans was very clear. Pitching coach Mel Stottlemyre had gone to the clubhouse to ask Rivera if he really was able to pitch, and although Rivera had not eaten or slept, he said, "I'm fine. I'm ready to go." Forty minutes after he began his warm-up, Rivera had retired the Red Sox, and the Yankees had won the game 10-7. Fans in his hometown watched, too, and at least some of the people who had wept with him earlier that day cheered him that night, the shouts of delight when he saved the win audible between the small houses of his hometown.

Rivera said afterward, "The most difficult part of my day was leaving my family, knowing they are still in pain. It was tough coming on that plane alone. . . . There's tears coming out of my eyes . . . but I have a job to do and I have 24 players that were waiting for me." He was touched by the response from his teammates and his fans. "I know this is home," he said. "This is my family. Brothers, fathers, Joe, my teammates. To see the fans, it was special. I can't be thankful enough for what everybody has done for me." Joe Torre, whose brother Rocco had died during the 1996 season, understood that the responsibility to play might actually be a relief to Rivera. It could give him "a chance to hide for an hour or so," because he would have to concentrate on his pitching.

Despite Rivera's unusual ability to shut his mind to everything but pitching, he had trouble focusing. "Even in the ballpark, there are moments when I go blank," he said. He slept until noon the day after the game and then called his family in Panama every hour. That night he closed out the Yankees' second win in the series. He said that the only time he did not think of the family's tragedy was when he was on the pitcher's mound. When the Yankees won Game 3 by 19-8 in Fenway

Mariano Rivera wiped away tears during a funeral service in Panama for his wife's cousin, Victor Dario Avila, and Avila's son. The two died in an accident at the Riveras' home in Puerto Caimito, Panama. After the funeral on October 12, 2004, Rivera flew back to the United States to pitch in the American League Championship Series.

Park, it seemed that they were heading for another World Series.

Then, in Game 4, Rivera was called in to protect a 4-3 lead in the eighth inning. He allowed one hit before retiring the side. All the Yankees needed were three more outs. In the ninth inning, though, Rivera walked Kevin Millar and the pinch runner stole second and scored on a single to tie the game. Boston won in the twelfth inning. In Game 5, Rivera was called in to pitch in the eighth inning, with runners on first and third bases and no outs, and let the Red Sox tie the game on a sacrifice fly. The Red Sox won in the fourteenth inning. Boston went on to win the American League Championship Series, taking the last two games, 11-6 and 10-3. It was the first time a team had come back from a three-game deficit in a postseason series. Jeter said, "It's not the same team." Although the loss of the series was not Rivera's fault, his unusual postseason failures had kept the Red Sox alive. Rivera's performance had again been the difference between winning and losing a series.

The winter of 2004–2005 would be different for Rivera and his family than any earlier one. Instead of going to Panama for a month at Christmas, Rivera paid to have more than 30 family members come to the United States. The big house in Panama was put up for sale. They had been proud of it, but now it would be a source of terrible memories. Even Rivera's winter preparation for the baseball season was different. Instead of working out at Yankee Stadium, Rivera lifted weights and rode a stationary bike at home. He did not throw a ball all winter. Instead he took time off. "I felt like I need it," he said.

2005

Although Rivera felt fine at spring training after his winter off, he blew his first two saves of the season against Boston. When he next appeared, the Boston fans cheered him, an irony he dealt with by politely tipping his hat to them. He said that it would be a silly thing to get upset about. In the second loss, Rivera had given up five runs in the ninth inning (four of them unearned runs on an error by Alex Rodriguez) and then loaded the bases. Joe Torre had to remove Rivera from the game. The Yankee fans then *booed* Rivera as he left the mound. No one could remember this happening before. Joe Torre said it was "inexcusable. . . . They wouldn't be champing at the bit to get to this ballpark if it wasn't for him." Commentators immediately began to ask if Rivera was over the hill as a closer. He had blown six of his last 11 chances against the Red Sox.

As had always happened before when Rivera faltered and commentators and fans began to predict his downfall, he came back strong. The 2005 season would turn out to be the best of his career. His ERA was a career-low 1.38 in 71 games. He achieved 43 saves in 47 opportunities (his 31 in a row over a period of four months was a career record), and he got the save in the All-Star Game. He came in ninth in the voting for the Most Valuable Player in the American League. He was second (the highest he had ever been) in the voting for the Cy Young Award. That year's Cy Young winner, Angels starting pitcher Bartolo Colón, said he had won the award because of skills that Rivera had taught him. Rivera also won the DHL Delivery Man of the Year award and MLB.com's Closer of the Year award. The Yankees won their eighth American League East title in a

★ ★ ★ ★ ★ ★
HOW RIVERA PREPARES MENTALLY FOR GAMES

Mariano Rivera arrives at 5:15 P.M. for a 7 P.M. game. Early on, he will watch the game in progress on TV in the clubhouse. He is checking to see how the umpire is calling strikes and balls. The strike zone has much more flexibility than casual viewers of baseball know, and everyone involved in the game needs to see where the zone is for that day. Rivera looks to see what pitches the Yankee pitcher is throwing and how the batters are hitting. Then Rivera has a massage. He jokes with the attendants. Sometimes he takes a nap. By the time he arrives in the bullpen, he has his game plan in mind.

row, and then lost the American League Division Series to the Los Angeles Angels of Anaheim.

After the 2005 season, players had to decide if they would compete in the inaugural World Baseball Classic, a competition among all-star teams from many countries that was being played in March 2006. Rivera made his Panamanian fans angry when he said he could not play for Panama. Rumors in Panama said that Rivera had called the team "incompetent," and the matter became a national scandal as Rivera was criticized in newspapers, on television, and in the streets. "They're ripping me apart," Rivera said. "It's like my head is in Haiti, my legs are in China." Rivera worked out over the winter, but no longer threw, protecting his arm and starting spring training slowly. He said he could not be ready to pitch in a series that would take place during spring training. It was a great blow for a country that idolizes Rivera, a place where he is so famous that he is sometimes waved through tollbooths for free.

2006 SEASON

Rivera struggled early in 2006, his ERA rising to 3.72 for April, but then he settled down, as usual. Rivera was not only named to the All-Star team, but he was told in advance that he would be its closer. His save in that game made him only the second pitcher (along with Dennis Eckersley) to have saved three All-Star Games.

As Rivera's career advanced, he began to approach some of the records that can only be achieved through longevity. On July 16, Rivera became only the fourth major-league player to record 400 saves. (The other three are Trevor Hoffman, who has 522 as of the end of the 2007 season; Lee Smith, with 478, and John Franco, with 424). Rivera got his 400 saves in fewer seasons than any of the others, and he had the lowest career ERA (2.32) among them. Although Rivera did not show that he knew this was a milestone, he said after the game that the mark was indeed special to him and that he planned to keep the ball

Catcher Joe Mauer of the Minnesota Twins congratulated Mariano Rivera after he got the save in the 2006 All-Star Game in Pittsburgh. The American League won the game, 3-2. Rivera is only the second pitcher who has earned saves in three All-Star Games.

rather than giving it to the Baseball Hall of Fame. "I want that one," he said. He gave them the cap he was wearing instead.

Rivera was on the disabled list early in September with an elbow strain. The Yankees were well ahead in the American

League East, and the decision was made to let him rest for most of the month. He had played enough games to earn the option on his contract with the Yankees that allowed him to pitch an extra year, through the end of the 2007 season. Then the Yankees failed to advance from the American League Division Series, losing to the Detroit Tigers. It was Rivera's first post-season without a save. He had had yet another successful year, posting a sub-2.00 ERA for the fourth year in a row, but he said, "I thought this was going to be our year."

8

2007 and Beyond: Rivera's Legacy

In February 2007, in New York's subways, seats of stunned-looking people could be seen reading (in several languages) headlines that said "Mo' Money" and "Show Me the Money!" In December, Mariano Rivera's agent had asked general manager Brian Cashman for a two-year extension of Rivera's contract, which would end after the 2007 season. The Yankees refused. Clearly they were waiting to see how well Rivera pitched in 2007 and how well his health held up. If the Yankees did not re-sign him by Opening Day, Rivera said he would not negotiate during the season but would become a free agent at the end of the postseason and consider all offers—even from the Red Sox.

In the past, Rivera had gone to arbitration over his contracts, but he had never threatened to leave the Yankees. Now he threatened to leave if not treated "with respect." Rivera had never worn anything but Yankee pinstripes, and he had always said that he wanted to finish his career as a Yankee and that he especially would never play for Boston.

In fact, Rivera was still saying that he would prefer to finish his career as a Yankee, and Cashman said, "He's the best and he'll still be the best [at the end of the season]. We'll get something done with him at the appropriate time." Since the Yankees did not offer to extend his contract before Opening Day, there would be no more discussion of the matter until the autumn.

TEAM LEADER

Teammates and fans had trouble imagining Rivera on another team or the team without Rivera. His presence on the mound had been a source of comfort for fans and teammates since 1995. Some of his teammates had known him since 1990 or '91. "Never a reason to sweat with Rivera," said a *Newsday* article in which Joe Torre, Derek Jeter, pitching coach Ron Guidry, and others spoke of how important Rivera had been to the team through the years. Jeter said he never worried about Rivera because he was so used to his being there. He joked that when Rivera was "50 or 60, he won't be able to do some of those things. But the way I look at it, even on Oldtimers' Day, Mo will be hard to hit."

As well as being an irreplaceable closer, Rivera had become a team leader. Originally, he was shy. The warmth was there, said Jeter, but it took you awhile to get to know him. In recent years, Rivera had mentored younger players, especially young Latino players and all pitchers. During spring training, Rivera would bring home all the young players for Clara to feed. Rivera told the young Latino players to learn English (as he hadn't) and to stay out of trouble—"don't get caught up with New York City. Because New York City will stand and you will go." For those who are interested, he spoke about his religious beliefs. He startled young players with his approachability. The young catcher Wil Nieves was amazed when the famous player introduced himself during spring training. "We talk a little about everything. I think he's a better human being than he is a pitcher." That's saying a lot.

During the regular season, Rivera's locker—since 2007, the locker that was once Bernie Williams's—was a place for players to gather before the game. "This is the hot corner—*la esquina caliente,*" reliever Luis Vizcaíno said. It wasn't just the younger players who found Rivera inspiring, on and off the pitcher's mound. "He comes in here and picks everybody up," said Jorge Posada, who has played with Rivera since the minor leagues. "He's always got a smile on his face, and people out there don't see that. In the clubhouse, he's completely different than the guy people see on the mound. He's a great friend and a great person." After the 2006 season, Rivera even gave a pep talk to the New Jersey Nets, about "good times" and "hard times" and the importance of team members supporting one another.

DINNER AT MO'S

During the 2006 season, Rivera did something that gave fans a chance to see a more relaxed side of him: He opened a restaurant called Mo's New York Grill, in New Rochelle, New York, where he lived for many years. His partners include Brandon Steiner, CEO of Steiner Sports, the sports memorabilia company, and the family of chef Gary Fosina. The chef is the son of Joe Fosina, who has been in charge of Yankee uniform alterations since the 1970s. When Rivera needed a way in 1995 to get from his apartment in New Rochelle to Yankee Stadium for his first appearance in the major leagues, he called Fosina.

Over time, the Riveras and the Fosinas became like family to each other. Joe Fosina and his wife visited the Riveras in Panama, and when the Yankees were playing at home over the Fourth of July, the Riveras would go to the barbecue at the Fosinas' house. Their son Gary cooked, because he was a chef.

In 2006, Mariano Rivera opened a restaurant, Mo's New York Grill, in New Rochelle, New York. Here, he stands in the restaurant's hallway, filled with photos of famous moments in Yankee history. His demand for excellence on the ball field is also evident in his restaurant.

Joe used to tease them, "When are you going to open a restaurant?" Now they have.

For fans of Rivera, there are two remarkable things about Mo's New York Grill. One is that, when Rivera is there, he walks around, sometimes with his family, chatting and asking customers if they like their food. It is the open, friendly side of a man whom baseball fans usually see only when he has his game face on.

The other thing to notice is how much Rivera's attitude about the restaurant resembles his attitude about pitching. He's famous, sure, and that will get people to come eat there—once. After that, he said, people will come back only if the food is good. It's in the attention to detail and that demand for excellence that the restaurant represents Rivera's values. It also represents his taste. He wanted a family restaurant, not a sports bar. Although professional restaurant designers helped create the restaurant, Rivera chose to install a huge saltwater fish tank. It is there partly in honor of his father's work and partly because he likes fish and travels too much to have a tank at home. There's a Panamanian special on the menu. Rivera also made some other choices about the décor. There are only a few televisions. There is a large painting of Rivera near the front door, but there is also a picture of the "Joseph Fosina Field House" at City Park in New Rochelle, honoring Joe Fosina's many years of work with the local youth football program. Most of the Yankees pictures are down a hall and in a back dining room, so the restaurant does not feel like a Yankee theme park. And Rivera specified that only pictures of past teams should be displayed, because the team roster changes often and he did not want part of his current team to be honored and part not. He did not want to hurt anyone's feelings. As usual, Rivera paid attention to details.

2007 SEASON

Early in 2007, the Yankees slid into a sub-.500 pit that more or less coincided with a slump by Rivera, who finished the month of April with a 10.57 ERA. As the season continued, Rivera would settle down after his shaky start. On July 14, he earned his 425th career save, passing John Franco for third place on the all-time saves list. From May to August, Rivera's ERA was 1.47. But for the first time since becoming a closer, he would finish the season with an ERA over 3.00. He was also not invited to the All-Star Game.

Among the other Yankees, Posada and Jeter continued to have two of the highest batting averages in the league. Alex Rodriguez tied the record for home runs in April. He faltered a bit in May and early June but came back to be the hitter—including the clutch hitter—that he had always meant to be.

Still, for the Yankees, 2007 was a disappointment. Although they fought back in the second half of the season to come with 1½ games of the Red Sox, the Yankees failed to win the American League East title for the first time since 1997. The team did make the play-offs as the wild-card team and faced the Cleveland Indians in the American League Division Series. Rivera pitched 4²/₃ scoreless innings and lowered his

★ ★ ★ ★ ★ ★

NO. 42

On April 15, 2007, Major League Baseball celebrated the sixtieth anniversary of Jackie Robinson's debut as the first African-American player on a major-league team. All major-league players and managers were invited to wear his number, No. 42, on that day. Hundreds did.

Rivera was the only player who could wear his own number and still honor Robinson. He was assigned No. 42 in 1995. On April 15, 1997, when the number was retired across the major leagues (ordinarily a number is retired only by the player's own team), Rivera found out that his number was the same as Jackie Robinson's. At the time, players who were wearing the number were allowed to keep it. Rivera is the last remaining major leaguer to have No. 42. He said, "Especially for a minority player like me, being the last one to wear number 42 is an honor, and I do carry it with honor."

lifetime postseason ERA to 0.77, but the Yankees failed to make it out of the first round, winning only one postseason game.

THE END OF AN ERA

Yankees owner George Steinbrenner said during the play-offs that, if the Yankees did not win, he would fire manager Joe Torre. It was a flash of the old Steinbrenner, who threatened and fired and raged. Brian Cashman had been responsible for hirings and firings all year. Cashman and Steinbrenner's sons, Hank and Hal, who had become more involved in the team's operations as their father had gotten older, would meet with George Steinbrenner after the season to make decisions about the team.

And there was plenty in flux in the off-season. Rivera and catcher Jorge Posada were free agents. Andy Pettitte, who had returned to the team in 2007 after an exile to the Houston Astros, was deciding if he wanted to play for the Yankees or retire. There was a possibility that only Derek Jeter would be left from the 1996 championship team. Somewhat overshadowing these matters was the question of whether Alex Rodriguez, the winner of the league's MVP award, his third, would opt to become a free agent. A-Rod's agent, Scott Boras, announced in the middle of Game 4 of the World Series that Rodriguez would seek other offers.

As the Yankees' old foe, Boston, went on to win its second World Series in four years, the future of the New York team occupied fans' minds. The Steinbrenners offered Joe Torre a contract that cut his salary by $2 million but included a bonus of $1 million for each round of the postseason that the team reached. The offer was an insult, suggesting that Torre would manage the team better in the postseason if he had a financial incentive to do so. Torre turned it down, accepting an offer to manage the Los Angeles Dodgers.

The determination continues. Mariano Rivera was on the mound again, this time in the ninth inning of a game on July 15, 2007, against the Tampa Bay Devil Rays. The Yankees won, 7-6, and Rivera earned the 426th save of his career. He was in sole possession of third place on the career saves list.

The Yankees named Joe Girardi as their new manager. Girardi was not the sentimental favorite, but he had been a catcher with the Yankees on their 1996, 1998, and 1999 World Champion teams. He was the National League Manager of the Year in 2006, when he kept the rookie-laden Florida Marlins in contention for much of the season.

Rodriguez then agreed to a deal with the Yankees. Teams had not lined up to make him a better offer. The *New York Times* reported that Rivera had stayed in touch with Rodriguez, urging him to return to the Yankees. Rodriguez told the press, "Mariano is obviously someone we can't live without, because he's one of a kind and he's so unique in what he does for us. And he's such an unbelievable force in our clubhouse."

Posada also agreed to a new contract with the Yankees. And in mid-November, Rivera said he would accept the Yankees' three-year, $45 million contract offer. The deal was higher than the $39 million he had originally been offered, but he was not able to get a guaranteed fourth year, as Posada had. Still, the contract made him the highest-paid closer in history and gave him a contract through age 41.

"We've got everybody back," Hank Steinbrenner told The Associated Press. This wasn't quite true. It was the end of the Joe Torre era. But Rivera would get his wish to finish his career as a New York Yankee. He, Posada, and Jeter would have another chance to try to re-create the magic of the 1996–2000 Yankees.

THE FUTURE

After the annual scare about a Rivera slump in 2007, he recovered and returned to his usual reliability. In an article by Jayson Stark called "The Pitch that Scares Major Leaguers," Rivera's cutter was tied with Trevor Hoffman's changeup as the number-one pitch that batters did not want to face. Not bad for a 37-year-old closer.

Still, even Rivera will not be able to pitch forever. He will retire, not because others panic but because he no longer "trusts his stuff." "I don't like to think about that," he said in 2006. "I'll have to think about it soon enough. Everyone gets old. Everyone's time comes eventually. Mine will, I know that. But I won't worry about that until it happens. I don't think it's going to happen for some time, but, really, only God knows that, right?" There is little doubt that after retirement, Rivera will continue to be involved with young baseball players, with some sort of Christian ministry, and with charity work, both in Panama and in the United States. He looks forward to spending more time with his family.

Rivera's retirement is not something his team or his fans like to think about, either. Other closers have posted better numbers for a short time (Eric Gagné, for instance). Goose Gossage has said that it isn't right to call Rivera the best closer of all time, because when Gossage closed, the role was different. Gossage pitched more innings and was more likely to be called in with men on base. Still, Yankee fans are not the only ones who say there is only one Mariano. He has been consistently good over a long career, and no one questions his status as the best postseason closer of all time. When Rivera is inducted into the Baseball Hall of Fame, five years after he retires, he will be one of the few relief pitchers to be given that honor.

No doubt, Rivera will be pleased. He has said so, a bit shyly, not wanting to take his induction for granted. But it seems unlikely that his winning statistics are the part of his legacy he will value most. His deep desire to win has always been balanced by his desire to be a good teammate, friend, and family and community member. Those values did not come just from his background as a poor boy who became successful. Lots of rich athletes started poor. They did not come just from his religion. Although Rivera is strengthened by his belief in God, religious beliefs can make people self-righteous or dismissive toward people who believe differently.

Rivera has a combination of extreme self-confidence and extreme humility. He has always taken responsibility for his mistakes and not looked to put the blame on others. He has wanted to be someone people could count on, and has been, and he has valued excellence over fame. It shows in his pitching, in his restaurant, in how he has given to others, and in how he treats the people around him. He wants that responsibility because it gives him as much control as any human being can have. He will do the best he can, and the rest he leaves up to God.

Rivera believes that he has a responsibility greater even than saving games. "As long as I can help somebody, I'm happy," he says. Whether he's pitching a ball or signing a baseball card for a fan, he gives the matter his complete attention. "He's the best I've ever been around," Joe Torre said of Rivera. "Not only the ability to pitch and perform under pressure, but the calm he puts over the clubhouse." He likes to do things right. That has been his gift to his team and his fans.

STATISTICS

MARIANO RIVERA
Primary position: Pitcher

Full name: Mariano Rivera •
Born: November 29, 1969, Panama City,
Panama • Height: 6'2" • Weight: 185 lbs. •
Team: New York Yankees (1995–present)

YEAR	TEAM	G	W	L	SV	BB	SO	ERA
1995	NYY	19	5	3	0	30	51	5.51
1996	NYY	61	8	3	5	34	130	2.09
1997	NYY	66	6	4	43	20	68	1.88
1998	NYY	54	3	0	36	17	36	1.91
1999	NYY	66	4	3	45	18	52	1.83
2000	NYY	66	7	4	36	25	58	2.85
2001	NYY	71	4	6	50	12	83	2.34
2002	NYY	45	1	4	28	11	41	2.74
2003	NYY	64	5	2	40	10	63	1.66
2004	NYY	74	4	2	53	20	66	1.94
2005	NYY	71	7	4	43	18	80	1.38
2006	NYY	63	5	5	34	11	55	1.80
2007	NYY	67	3	4	30	12	74	3.15
TOTAL		787	62	44	443	238	857	2.35

Key: NYY = New York Yankees; G = Games; W = Wins; L = Losses; SV = Saves;
BB = Bases on balls; SO = Strikeouts; ERA = Earned run average

CHRONOLOGY

1969   **November 29** Born in a Panama City, Panama, hospital to a family living in Puerto Caimito, Panama.

1990   **February 17** Signs contract to play for the New York Yankees.

1990–1995   Plays on minor-league teams in the Yankee farm system.

1991   **November 9** Marries Clara.

1992   **August 27** Has elbow surgery.

1995   **May 23** Makes his major-league debut.

1996   First full year in the major leagues; breaks Yankee record for strikeouts by a reliever (130); Yankees win World Series; is third in voting for the Cy Young Award; receives the Buck Canel Award from the Baseball Writers' Association of America as top Latin American player of the year.

1997   Becomes closer for Yankees; learns to throw cut fastball; makes the All-Star team and saves game for the American League; wins *Sporting News* Reliever of the Year Award.

1998   Yankees win the World Series; Rivera earns his first World Series save.

1999   Makes the All-Star team; Yankees win the World Series; Rivera is named the World Series MVP, is third in voting for the Cy Young Award; wins the American League Rolaids Relief Man of the Year Award, the Babe Ruth Award, and the *Sporting News* Reliever of the Year Award.

2000   Makes the All-Star team; Yankees win third consecutive World Series; Rivera becomes the first pitcher to record the last out in three consecutive World Series; moves family from Panama to Westchester County, New York.

2001   Makes the All-Star team; wins the American League
Rolaids Relief Man of the Year Award (dedicates award
to New York City Fire Department); receives the
Sporting News Reliever of the Year Award.

2002   Makes the All-Star team; is placed on the disabled list
three times.

2003   Is named the American League Championship Series
MVP; receives the Thurman Munson Award (for
charitable works).

2004   Makes the All-Star team; is third in voting for Cy
Young Award; wins the American League Rolaids
Relief Man of the Year Award and the *Sporting News*

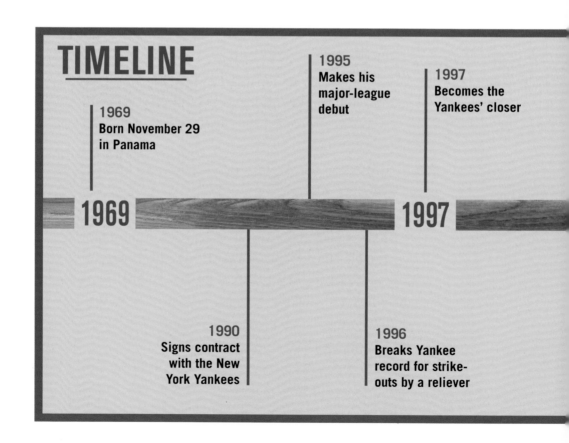

TIMELINE

1995
Makes his
major-league
debut

1997
Becomes the
Yankees' closer

1969
Born November 29
in Panama

1969

1997

1990
Signs contract
with the New
York Yankees

1996
Breaks Yankee
record for strike-
outs by a reliever

Reliever of the Year Award; two family members die in an accident at his house in Panama.

2005 Makes the All-Star team and saves game for the American League; is second in voting for the Cy Young Award; named New York Yankees Player of the Year; wins the American League Rolaids Relief Man of the Year Award, the *Sporting News* Reliever of the Year Award, the DHL Delivery Man of the Year, and the MLB.com Closer of the Year Award.

2006 **June 20** Has his first major-league at-bat (strikes out).

July 16 Becomes the fourth major-league pitcher to record 400 saves.

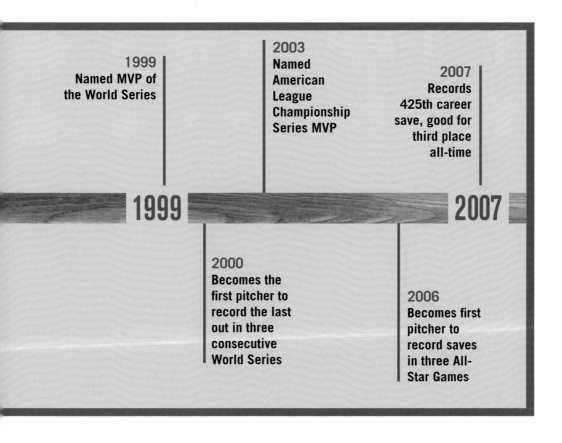

1999
Named MVP of
the World Series

2003
Named
American
League
Championship
Series MVP

2007
Records
425th career
save, good for
third place
all-time

1999 ———————————— **2007**

2000
Becomes the
first pitcher to
record the last
out in three
consecutive
World Series

2006
Becomes first
pitcher to
record saves
in three All-
Star Games

Makes the All-Star team and saves game for the American League—first pitcher to record three saves in All-Star Game; wins DHL Delivery Man of the Year and MLB.com Closer of the Year Award.

2007   **July 14** Passes John Franco for third place in all-time saves, recording his 425th career save. Agrees to a three-year, $45 million contract with the New York Yankees.

GLOSSARY

arbitration The process by which a third party settles a salary dispute between a player and a team. In baseball, the player and the team each submit a salary figure to the arbitrator. After comparing the player to similar players, the arbitrator decides what his salary will be—choosing either the figure submitted by the player or the one submitted by the team.

at-bat An official turn at batting that is charged to a baseball player, except when the player walks, sacrifices, is hit by a pitched ball, or is interfered with by a catcher. At-bats are used to calculate a player's batting average and slugging percentage.

ball A pitch that does not pass over home plate in the strike zone. A batter who receives four balls gets a walk.

baseball commissioner The highest-ranking office in Major League Baseball.

brushback pitch A pitch intentionally thrown close to a batter to intimidate him, or "brush him back" from the plate.

bullpen The area where pitchers warm up, usually behind the outfield fences. The name comes from its similarity to the place where bulls are kept before a bullfight.

bunt A ball that is deliberately not fully hit, with the batter either intending to get to first base before the infielder can field the ball or allowing a runner on base to advance.

catcher The defensive player directly behind home plate, whose job is to signal to the pitcher which kind of pitch to throw and where to throw it. This player also catches the pitch. Good catchers know hitters' strengths and weaknesses and can "frame" their catches to influence umpires to call more strikes.

changeup A slow pitch thrown with the same motion as a fastball in order to deceive the batter.

closer   A relief pitcher who is consistently used to "close" or finish the game by getting the final outs.

curveball   A pitch that curves on its way to home plate, thanks to the spin the pitcher places on the ball as he releases it.

cutter   A pitch that approaches home plate in a straight line, but then drops, or cuts, sharply toward or away from the hitter.

earned run average (ERA)   The statistic that indicates the average number of earned runs that a pitcher gives up in a nine-inning game. It is computed by multiplying the total number of earned runs by nine and dividing by the number of innings pitched.

error   When a defensive player makes a mistake that results in a runner reaching base or advancing a base, an error is designated by the game's scorer.

farm teams   The minor-league teams that provide young players with experience, with the expectation that successful players will move to the major leagues.

fastball   A high-velocity pitch that may have little movement; it is the most common type of pitch.

full count   A count of three balls and two strikes. Another strike results in a strikeout while another ball results in a walk.

games behind   A statistic used in team standings. It is figured by adding the difference in wins between a trailing team and the leader to the difference in losses, and dividing in two. So a team that is three games behind may trail by three in the win column and three in the loss column, or four and two, or any other combination of wins and losses totaling six.

MVP   The Most Valuable Player award (commonly known as the MVP) is an annual award given to one outstanding player in each league (American and National) of Major

League Baseball. The award is determined by the Baseball Writers' Association of America.

perfect game A special no-hitter in which a pitcher retires each batter consecutively, allowing no base runners through walks, errors, or any other means.

rubber game A term used for the fifth game of a five-game series or the seventh game of a seven-game series when the two teams have split the first four or six games, respectively.

sacrifice A ball hit by the batter that advances a runner to the next base while the batter receives an "out" for his attempt. Examples include a sacrifice fly and a sacrifice bunt.

save A statistic credited to a pitcher who comes into the game with his team leading and completes the game without giving up the lead. The pitcher must be the last pitcher in the game and must fulfill at least one of the following conditions: He comes into the game with a lead of no more than three runs and pitches at least one full inning; he comes into the game with the potential tying or winning run on base, at bat, or on deck; he pitches effectively for at least three innings after entering the game.

setup reliever A relief pitcher who is consistently used before the closer.

slider A relatively fast pitch with a slight curve in the opposite direction of the throwing arm.

strike A pitch that is swung at and missed or a pitch that is in the strike zone and is not swung at. A foul ball counts as a strike unless it would be the third strike. Three strikes and the batter is out.

strike zone The area directly over home plate up to the batter's chest (roughly where the batter's uniform lettering is) and down to his or her knees. Different umpires have slightly different strike zones, and players only ask that they be consistent.

BIBLIOGRAPHY

Abraham, Peter. "Rivera Gets 400th Save." *Westchester Journal News.* July 17, 2006.

Angell, Roger. *Game Time: A Baseball Companion.* New York: Harcourt Inc., 2003.

Antonen, Mel. "Yanks' Rivera Continues to Learn." *USA Today.* Oct. 9, 2006.

Bamberger, Michael. "Strikeouts by the Boatload." *Sports Illustrated.* March 24, 1997.

Cairns, Bob. *Pen Men: Baseball's Greatest Bullpen Stories Told by the Men Who Brought the Game Relief.* New York: St. Martin's Press, 1992.

Caldera, Pete. "Closer Teaches Younger Players the Ropes." *The Record.* March 31, 2006.

Chass, Murray. "Rivera's Injury Magnifies Bullpen Trouble." *New York Times.* July 21, 2002.

Curry, Jack. "Closing Thoughts: Rivera Remains the Infallible One." *New York Times.* October 29, 2000.

———. "Family Ordeal Only Strengthens Rivera's Faith." *New York Times.* March 12, 2003.

———. "Fear Drove Rivera to Relocate His Family Here." *New York Times.* March 10, 2005.

———. "Love of God Outweighs Love of the Game." *New York Times.* December 10, 1999.

———. "Rivera May Have Said Final Goodbye to Columbus." *New York Times.* July 5, 1995.

———. "Rivera's Final Pitch: Gone, Never Forgotten." *New York Times.* November 6, 2001.

———. "Set Up for the Pressure of Being the Yanks' Closer." *New York Times.* January 5, 1997.

Ettkin, Brian. "Once the Toast, Now the Toasted." *Albany Times Union.* April 7, 2005.

Euchner, Charles. *The Last Nine Innings*. Naperville, Ill.: Sourcebooks, 2006.

Feinsand, Mark. "Rivera Has Some Fun with Sox Fans." MLB.com. April 11, 2005.

———. "Yankees Players Awed by Rivera." MLB.com July 16, 2006.

Frias, Carlos. "Rivera Relishes Role as Yankees' Anchor." *Palm Beach Post*. April 19, 2007.

"Grieving Mariano Admits: I Go Blank on Mound." *New York Post*. October 17, 2004.

Hamill, Pete, ed. *The Subway Series Reader*. New York: Simon & Schuster, 2000.

Harper, John and Bob Klapisch. *Champions!: The Saga of the 1996 New York Yankees*. New York: Random House, 1996.

Harrington, Mike. "Rivera to the Rescue: Grief-Stricken Pitcher Saves Yankees in Opener." *Buffalo News*. October 13, 2004.

Howard, Johnette. "Mo's Expressions Worrisome." *Newsday*. May 9, 2007.

Jackson, Eric. "Running with the Pack." *Panama News*. October 17–November 6, 2004. Available online at http://www.thepanamanews.com/pn/v_10/issue_20/review_01.html.

Kepner, Tyler. "Rivera's 42 is Far More Than a Number to Him." *New York Times*, April 12, 2007.

Kernan, Kevin. "Mo Goes from Closer to Setup Man at Steak Eatery with Pal." *New York Post*. Oct. 27, 2006.

King, George. *Unbeatable! The Historic Season of the 1998 World Champion New York Yankees*. New York: HarperCollins, 1998.

King, George, and Joel Sherman. "Mo Money—or Else!" *New York Post*. Feb. 15, 2007.

Kinkhabwala, Aditi. "Mariano Cuts Path to Fame." *Albany Times Union.* July 16, 2006.

McCarron, Anthony. "Mo: Save the Worry." *Daily News.* May 9, 2007.

McKinley, James C. "Sorrow, and Questions, in a Land of Dreams." *New York Times.* October 16, 2004.

Murray, Noah K. "Best of the Best: From Humble Beginnings, Rivera Has Been Simply Divine." *Star-Ledger.* October 20, 2000.

New York Times. Champions: The 1998 New York Yankees. New York: Bishop Books, 1998.

New York Times. The New York Yankees Illustrated History. New York: St. Martin's, 2002.

"'Nuf Said: Mo Trusts His Stuff." *New York Post.* June 5, 2002.

O'Brien, Kat. "Never a Reason to Sweat with Rivera." *Newsday.* March 14, 2007.

O'Dwyer, Kieran. "A Cutter Above." *Sporting News.* July 27, 2006.

Olney, Buster. "The Confidence Man: Inside the Mind of Baseball's Greatest Closer, Mariano Rivera." *New York Magazine.* June 28, 2004.

———. *The Last Night of the Yankee Dynasty: The Game, the Team, and the Cost of Greatness.* New York: HarperCollins, 2004.

———. "Rivera Loses Ruling on Salary, But Takes It in Stride." *New York Times.* February 20, 2000.

Pedulla, Tom. "Yankees' Rivera Has Finishing Touch." *USA Today.* October 25, 1999.

Pierce, Charles P. and Elizabeth Einstein. "The Hammer of God." *Esquire.* June 2001.

"Robbin' Rivera All But Seals His Fate; Fessin' Up Not Enough to Save His Career." *New York Post.* March 13, 2002.

"Rubén's Crime Unforgivable." NorthJersey.com. March 13, 2002.

Schechter, Gabriel. "A Closer Look: The Evolution of the Closer." National Baseball Hall of Fame. Available online at http://www.baseballhalloffame.org/library/columns/gs_060118.htm.

Sherman, Joel. *Birth of a Dynasty: Behind the Pinstripes with the 1996 Yankees.* Emmaus, Pa.: Rodale Press, 2006.

Stark, Jayson. "The Pitches that Scare Major Leaguers." ESPN.com. May 15, 2007. Available online at http://ESPN .go.com/mlb/columns/stark_jayson/1382666.html.

"Sultan of Save: Rivera's Earned Place Among Yankee Legends." *New York Post.* June 27, 2007.

"Support Touches Mariano." *New York Post.* October 14, 2004.

Vecsey, George. "Rivera Puts Mistake Behind Him, as He Always Does." *New York Times.* May 21, 2006.

Verducci, Tom. "Gotta Get to Mo." *Sports Illustrated.* June 1, 2004.

———. "The Yanks Allowed the Red Sox Their Day of Fenway Glory, Then Dispatched Boston to Resume Their Inexorable March Back to the World Series." *Sports Illustrated.* October 25, 1999.

Walker, Ben. "Rivera No Longer Mr. Automatic." *Albany Times Union.* May 7, 2002.

Wikipedia. "Mariano Rivera." Available online at http://en.wikepedia.org/wiki/Mariano_Rivera.

Wikipedia. "The New York Yankees." Available online at http://en.wikepedia.org/wiki/New_York_Yankees.

Wojnarowski, Adrian. "Mariano Rivera Is Still a Mystery to Some." ESPN.com. October 26, 2001.

FURTHER READING

New York Times. The New York Yankees Illustrated History. New York: St. Martin's, 2002.

Sherman, Joel. *Birth of a Dynasty: Behind the Pinstripes with the 1996 Yankees.* Emmaus, Pa.: Rodale Press, 2006.

Stout, Glenn. *New York Yankees: Yesterday and Today.* Lincolnwood, Ill.: Publications International, 2007.

————. *Yankees Century: 100 Years of New York Yankees Baseball.* Boston: Houghton Mifflin, 2002.

Tan, Cecilia. *The 50 Greatest Yankee Games.* Hoboken, N.J.: John Wiley & Sons, 2005.

Vancil, Mark. *The Greatest Yankee Teams.* New York: Ballantine Books, 2004.

Votano, Paul. *Late and Close: A History of Relief Pitching.* Jefferson, N.C.: McFarland & Company, 2002.

Wendel, Tim. *The New Face of Baseball: The One-Hundred-Year Rise and Triumph of Latinos in America's Favorite Sport.* New York: Rayo, 2003.

WEB SITES

Baseball Almanac
http://www.baseball-almanac.com

Baseball Reference
http://www.baseball-reference.com

Major League Baseball: The Official Site
http://mlb.mlb.com

The Official Site of the New York Yankees
http://yankees.mlb.com

An Unofficial Mariano Rivera Fan Club Site
http://marianorivera.com

PHOTO CREDITS

INDEX

Albany-Colonie Yankees, 23
All-Star Games, 46, 54, 105
   years in, 59, 97, 98
Alomar, Roberto, 44
Alomar, Sandy, Jr., 60
American League
   championship series, 49–50, 65,
     66, 77, 91, 92–96
   division series, 28–30, 34, 48–49,
     59–60, 65, 75–77, 88, 91, 92,
     96, 98, 100, 106–107
   MVPs, 53, 97, 107
Anaheim Angels, 88, 98
Anderson, Dave, 84
Angell, Roger, 41
Arizona Diamondbacks, 35, 75
   and the World Series, 7, 77–82,
     84–86
Atlanta Braves, 59, 62
   and the World Series, 50–51, 53,
     65
Avery, Steve, 50
Avila, Victor Dario, 92–93

Baltimore Orioles, 44–45, 49–50
baseball
   commissioner, 32
   fans, 5, 16, 31, 38–39, 49–50,
     52–53, 56, 67–68, 73, 75, 77,
     79–80, 82, 85, 92, 93–94, 96–
     97, 102–104, 107, 110–111
   Latinos in, 22, 24–25, 102
   scouts, 4, 15–17, 27, 34, 85
   strikes, 34, 38, 72
Bellán, Esteban Enrique, 24
Bell, Jay, 82
Berra, Yogi, 32
Blitzer, Billy, 4
Blowers, Mike, 30, 66
Boggs, Wade, 34, 37, 51
Boone, Aaron, 91, 92
Boras, Scott, 107
Boston Red Sox, 57, 63, 101–102,
   106
   games against, 46, 91, 92–96,
     97
   and the World Series, 92, 107
Brooklyn Dodgers, 42, 66
Brosius, Scott, 73, 79, 80, 82, 84, 88

Bush, George W., 78
Butterfield, Brian, 22

Cairns, Bob
   Pen Men, 5
Carew, Rod, 10, 25
Caribbean Series, 17
Cashman, Brian
   and the Yankees, 26–27, 60, 62,
     101–102, 107
Castro, Fidel, 16–17
Castro, Luis, 24
Chicago White Sox, 43, 45, 73
Clemens, Roger, 78
Cleveland Indians
   games against, 59–60, 87, 92,
     106–107
Colón, Bartolo, 97
Colorado Rockies, 22
Columbus Clippers, 23–28
Cone, David
   teammate, 29–30, 34, 37, 39, 50,
     62, 80
Counsell, Craig, 82
Curry, Jack, 42–43, 66, 85
Cuza, Fernando, 68
Cymbala, Jim, 89
Cy Young Award, 53, 97

Damn Yankees (musical), 31
Damon, Johnny, 57
Dellucci, David, 82
Detroit Tigers, 26, 71, 100

Eckersley, Dennis, 98
Euchner, Charles
   The Last Nine Innings, 85
Evers, Bill, 26

Fingers, Rollie, 66
Florida Marlins, 22, 91, 109
Ford, Whitey, 22
Fosina, Gary, 103
Fosina, Joe, 103–105
Franco, John, 98, 105
Fuentes, Oscar, 17

Gagné, Eric, 110
Garcia, Richie, 49

Giambi, Jason, 91
Giambi, Jeremy, 75–76
Girardi, Joe, 37–38, 44, 53, 57, 80, 109
Gomez, Lefty, 5
Gonzalez, Luis, 82, 84
Gooden, Dwight, 37, 39
Gossage, Goose, 7, 30, 48, 56, 57, 110
Grace, Mark, 77, 82
Greensboro, North Carolina
    playing in, 20, 22, 26
Guidry, Ron, 22, 102
Guillén, Ozzie, 43
Gulf Coast League, 19–20, 26

Hayes, Charlie, 48, 51
Hermoso, Rafael, 42, 69
Hoffman, Trevor, 98, 109
Holtzman, Jerome, 78
Houston Astros, 107
Howe, Steve, 38–39
Hrabosky, Al, 5

Jeter, Derek
    teammate, 14, 19, 22, 23, 29, 34,
        37, 38, 44, 49, 55, 68, 72, 75–77,
        79, 82, 84, 88, 89, 92, 102, 107,
        109
Jobe, Frank, 22
Johnson, Randy, 29, 77
Jones, Chipper, 59

Kaat, Jim, 57
Kansas City Royals, 15, 39
Kelly, Tom, 7
Key, Jimmy, 37, 39, 51
Kim, Byung-Hyun, 79
King, George, 62
Klapisch, Bob, 45
Klesko, Ryan, 51
Knoblauch, Chuck
    teammate, 39, 45, 59, 67–68, 72,
        79–80, 88
Koufax, Sandy, 59

Last Nine Innings, The (Euchner), 85
Latin America
    baseball in, 10, 16–17
Leiter, Al, 57

Lemke, Mark, 51
Leyritz, Jim, 41, 44, 50
Llenas, Winston, 25
Lloyd, Graeme, 51, 63
Long, Terrence, 75
Los Angeles Dodgers, 31, 107
Lupica, Mike, 35, 81
Lyle, Sparky, 5

Maddux, Greg, 51
Maier, Jeffrey, 49
Mantle, Mickey, 56, 88
Manuel Amador Guerrero Order,
    66
Marberry, Fred, 42
Martínez, Pedro, 25
Martinez, Tino
    teammate, 37–38, 44–45, 72,
        79–80, 84–85, 88
Mattingly, Don, 34, 36
McCarver, Tim, 82
McLemore, Mark, 66
Mendoza, Ramiro, 57
Metallica
    "Enter Sandman," 7, 64, 94
Michael, Gene
    and the Yankees, 23, 26–27, 29,
        33–35
Millar, Kevin, 95
Miller, Damian, 82
Milwaukee Braves, 24
Minnesota Twins, 7, 41
    games against, 39, 91, 92
Molitor, Paul, 41
Monahan, Gene, 80
Mo's New York Grill, 103–105, 111
Mussina, Mike, 92

National Baseball Hall of Fame, 10,
    25, 91, 99, 110
National League, 50, 77
Negro Leagues, 24
Nelson, Jeff, 38–39, 48
New York Highlanders, 42
New York Mets, 66
New York Yankees
    1996 season, 35–39, 41–53, 55, 60,
        67, 88, 91, 94, 107, 109
    1999 season, 64–66, 109

2001 season, 35, 68–69, 72–73, 75–82, 84–86
2002 season, 87–89, 91
2003 season, 89–91
2004 season, 92–96
2005 season, 96–98
2006 season, 98–100, 103
2007 season, 1–8, 105–107, 109
contracts, 17–18, 32, 34, 37, 54–55, 68–69, 100, 101–102, 109
draft, 32
fans, 38–39, 49, 52–53, 56, 67–68, 73, 75, 77, 79–80, 82, 93–94, 96, 102, 104, 107, 110
managers and coaches, 1, 4, 7, 20, 22, 26, 32–39, 41–42, 44–46, 48, 50–51, 60, 64, 66, 79–81, 84, 94, 96, 102, 107, 109
minor leagues, 7, 19–20, 22–28, 33, 38, 103
owner, 32–37, 44, 60, 67, 85, 90–91, 107
players, 1, 7, 12, 14, 23, 34, 36–39, 41–42, 44–45, 48–51, 53, 54–55, 57, 62–64, 66, 67–68, 72–73, 75–82, 84–86, 88–89, 91, 102–103, 106, 107, 109
scouts, 15–17, 34
spring training, 1, 4, 22, 35, 37, 60, 88, 96, 98, 102–103
and the World Series, 7, 8, 31–32, 34–35, 49–53, 54, 59–60, 64, 65–66, 67, 75, 77–82, 84–86, 91, 92, 107, 109
Yankee Stadium, 7, 19, 31, 46, 49, 50, 64, 72, 73, 75, 77, 78–80, 92, 96, 103
Nieves, Wil, 103

Oakland A's, 66, 75–77
Olney, Buster, 55, 59, 60, 84
O'Neill, Paul
teammate, 37, 68, 73, 79–80, 88

Panama
baseball in, 9–10, 15, 98
charity in, 43, 62, 70, 110
childhood in, 9–15
home in, 22, 26, 53, 56, 66, 69–71, 93, 96, 103
Puerto Caimito in, 9, 10, 11
Pelé, 10

Pen Men (Cairns), 5
Pettitte, Andy
teammate, 19, 22, 23, 34, 37, 44–45, 48, 51, 80, 107
Philadelphia Athletics, 24, 51
Philadelphia Phillies, 24
Piazza, Mike, 66
Piniella, Lou, 77
pitching
closer, 3, 7, 38, 42–43, 49, 54–56, 59, 64, 69, 78, 92, 97–98, 102, 110
ERA, 1, 4, 20, 24, 26, 28, 29, 39, 41, 42, 46, 52, 63, 64, 77, 81, 89, 91, 97, 98, 100, 105, 107
fastball, 5, 7, 26–27, 41, 45, 57, 59, 109
in minor leagues, 19–20, 22–28
no-hitters, 20, 26, 57, 62
postseason, 28–30, 48–53, 59–60, 64–66, 77–82, 84–86, 93–96, 100, 106–107
relief, 3, 5, 7, 23, 24, 28, 39, 41–53, 59, 66, 78, 86, 103, 110
saves, 1, 3, 39, 42, 56, 59, 60, 64, 66, 77, 78, 81, 84, 88, 89, 91, 92, 96, 97, 98, 105
style, 3–5, 12–14, 16, 20, 22–23, 28, 30, 55, 59, 57, 66
Posada, Jorge
teammate, 19, 23, 27, 34, 37, 76, 88, 103, 106–107, 109

Raybourn, Herb, 15–17
Rickey, Branch, 42
Righetti, Dave, 88
Ripken, Cal, 44
Rivera, Alvaro (brother), 12
Rivera, Clara (wife), 18, 56, 102
family, 89, 92–93
marriage, 22
Rivera, Delia (mother), 10, 12, 70, 93
Rivera, Delia (sister), 12
Rivera, Giraldo (brother), 12
Rivera, Jafet (son), 56
Rivera, Jaziel (son), 89
Rivera, Mariano (father), 10
fisherman, 12, 14–15, 70, 105
influence, 12–14, 18
Rivera, Mariano
awards, 20, 66, 70, 86, 91, 92, 97
businesses, 103–105

childhood, 9–15, 55, 89
chronology, 113–116
education, 10, 14
faith, 8, 43, 62–63, 64, 81, 86, 89,
    102–103, 110–111
injuries, 22, 25, 27, 45, 46, 51, 84,
    87, 99
marriage, 22
retirement, 110
statistics, 112
Rivera, Mariano (son), 56
Rivera, Rubén (cousin)
    theft, 88
    and the Yankees, 12, 17, 22, 34, 88
Rizzo, Mike, 85
Robinson, Humberto, 24
Robinson, Jackie, 24, 42, 106
Rochester Red Wings, 26–27
Rodriguez, Alex
    teammate, 1, 91, 92, 96, 106, 107,
    109
Rogers, Kenny, 37, 39, 48
Ruth, Babe, 56, 92

San Diego Padres, 64, 88
Schilling, Curt, 75, 77–79, 81
Seattle Mariners
    games against, 28–30, 34, 66, 75,
    77
September 11, 2001, terrorist attacks
    and baseball, 72, 73, 75
    events of, 71–73, 86
Sheffield, Gary, 91
Sherlock, Glenn, 20
Sherman, Joel, 45
Showalter, Buck, 84
    and the Yankees, 26–28, 30,
    33–35
Smith, Claire, 41
Smith, Lee, 98
Sojo, Luis, 80, 93
Soriano, Alfonso, 79, 81, 91
Sosa, Sammy, 25
Spencer, Shane, 73, 76
Stanley, Mike, 34, 36–37
Stark, Jayson, 109
Steinbrenner, George
    Yankees owner, 32–37, 44, 60, 67,
    85, 90–91, 107
Steinbrenner, Hal, 107
Steinbrenner, Hank, 107, 109
Steiner, Brandon, 103

St. Louis Cardinals, 27, 50
Stottlemyre, Mel, 59, 94
Strawberry, Darryl, 64
Suzuki, Ichiro, 75

Texas Rangers, 48–49, 55, 65
Thome, Jim, 59
Torre, Frank, 35, 51
Torre, Joe, 109, 111
    Yankees manager, 1, 4, 35–36,
    37–38, 39, 41–42, 44–46, 48, 50,
    51, 60, 64, 66, 79–81, 84, 94, 96,
    102, 107
Torre, Rocco, 94
Troy Haymakers, 24
Turner, Ted, 50

Urbina, Ugueth, 71

Velarde, Randy, 37
Verducci, Tom, 53
Vincent, Fay, 32
Vizcaíno, Luis, 103

Washington Senators, 24, 31, 42
Watson, Bob, 35, 37–38, 44, 60
Weathers, David, 51
Wells, David, 26, 62, 63
Wetteland, John
    teammate, 27, 38, 39, 41–44, 48,
    51, 54–55, 59, 66
Wickman, Bob, 38, 39
Williams, Bernie
    teammate, 23, 34, 37, 39, 51, 66,
    72, 88, 103
Williams, Gerald, 45, 88
Wilson, Enrique, 86
Winfield, Dave, 32
Wohlers, Mark, 50
Womack, Tony, 82
World Baseball Classic, 98
World Series, 30, 35–36, 95
    1996 series, 50–53, 67, 88
    2001 series, 7, 77–82, 84–86, 89
    championships, 8, 31–32, 50–53,
    64–66, 67, 77–82, 84–86, 91
    MVP, 66
World War I, 72
World War II, 24

Zimmer, Don, 66, 81

ABOUT THE AUTHOR

JUDITH LEVIN has worked in publishing for 20 years as an editor and as a freelance writer. She is the author of a number of biographies, including one about Ichiro Suzuki, for Facts on File, as well as books for children and teens on history and science. Judith has been a baseball fan ever since she helped raise a catcher and saw the hard work, patience, and concentration that the game requires. She has been a Yankees fan for about the same length of time.